A truly inspirational memoir, this is Ed's story: an affecting, candid and wildly funny tale of one man's meteoric rise to the top of the retail and fashion world – from heroin addict to MD of Liberty, one of Britain's most iconic institutions.

Along the way Ed shares his ups and downs: the riotous hedonism of the 1980s New York and Florida party scene; the devastating impact of the AIDS crisis and the loss of his best friend; his first job at Macy's as a spritzer; his battle with drug addiction and depression; and working for high-profile stars. Above all he tells the story of transforming the fortunes of two of New York's most prestigious luxury department stores and of course, finally coming to London to take the reins at Liberty.

At Liberty is a window into a seemingly glamorous world, a world that Ed writes about with a spark, a fantastic sense of pathos and wry, self-deprecating humour. Ed truly is a larger-than-life character, on and off the page.

Before taking the top job at Liberty in 2008, Ed Burstell was Senior Vice President at Bergdorf Goodman and General Manager of upscale fashion accessories boutique Henri Bendel. Ed became known for his flamboyant and gregarious personality as the star of Channel 4's three-part *Liberty of London* documentary. Liberty now welcomes in excess of five million people from all over the world.

AT LIBERTY

from rehab to the front row

ED BURSTELL

Michael O'Mara Books Limited

First published in Great Britain in 2015 by
Michael O'Mara Books Limited
9 Lion Yard
Tremadoc Road
London SW4 7NQ

Papers used by Michael O'Mara Books Limited are natural, recyclable
products made from wood grown in sustainable forests. The
manufacturing processes conform to the environmental regulations
of the country of origin.

ISBN: 978-1-78243-468-9 in hardback print format
ISBN: 978-1-78243-469-6 in ebook format

1 2 3 4 5 6 7 8 9 10

Cover design by Simon Levy
Cover photographs by Nato Welton, inside photographs
from Ed Burstell, and the Channel 4 *Liberty of London* photo by
philfisk.com
Designed and typeset by Ana Bjezancevic
Printed and bound by CPI Group (UK) Ltd, Croydon, CR0 4YY

www.mombooks.com

For Mom and Dad

Contents

INTRODUCTION

For hundreds of millions of retail workers all over the world, from Walmart to Tesco to Bergdorf Goodman, retail can be one of the toughest grinds there is. In the luxury sector it is easy to fantasize about the lives of senior management who seem to waft in and out, always just back from some glamorous trip or fashion event. Behind the scenes, however, there can be more drama, scheming and backstabbing than any truly great soap opera.

So how does a relatively sane guy, who is also a relatively nice guy by nature, but with no connections, manage to make it to the top of a wildly competitive industry? This book details the ups and downs of the early days in Westchester, New York; the colourful, sometimes scandalous, antics of my European relatives; and my first taste of New York City, in one of its most infamous periods. Coming of age in late seventies and early eighties New York was an experience filled with dark glamour and excitement. Drugs were as commonplace as offering a beer to a neighbour at a suburban barbecue, and my experiences as an unknown were just as shocking as those of the celebrities of the day.

After the painful ordeal of rehab and losing my first true love to AIDS, I threw myself into work at the only place that would have me: as a fragrance sprayer at Macy's, Herald Square. This mind-numbing, and often hilarious, job gave me a small entrée into the enormous beauty industry, leading to positions at Neiman Marcus, and then as buyer at the legendary Bloomingdale's of the eighties, where the glamorous facade hid daily screaming, hysterics, and general mayhem! Through it all, I watched, learned, and persevered – discovering and launching some of the world's top beauty and fragrance lines that exist to this day, while making friends and enemies that would play a part in my life for years to come.

As the nineties began, I took on my biggest challenge yet, as the head buyer at Henri Bendel, then considered New York's most prestigious and exclusive store. But after the store was sold and bought, I weathered countless new leaders and new directives as the business floundered. Finally in 1998, as the last man standing after an expansion plan failed, I rose to the highest level in the store – general manager. But then what? The only working assets were a beautiful building, albeit bereft of customers, and staff frantically sending out résumés to avoid going down with the sinking ship.

In the seven years that followed, my team and I brought the store back from the dead, in a fascinating study of pre-internet marketing and merchandising savvy.

Finding a niche the larger stores had ignored, Bendel's truly became the *Sex and the City* store – full of colour, fun, life and, of course, plenty of parties, fêting everyone from Diane von Furstenberg to Rick Owens to Jay Z and Damon Dash to drag superstar, RuPaul. And never one to shy away from controversy, in 2000 there was probably no more (in)famous a woman in the country than Monica Lewinsky. After a chance meeting in a local supermarket, we became friends and I encouraged her ambition to start and launch a handbag line. The pandemonium and furore that ensued made the front pages of every newspaper.

Over several years the store went from strength to strength, with ever more launches and events; it heaved with hungry customers. But when the world's most successful luxury store, Bergdorf Goodman, called, it was time to go. After a $25,000 makeover to exchange my casual uniform of jeans and pullovers for the mandatory Bergdorf uniform of suits and ties, I leapt into the high-stakes world of Prada, Chanel, Hermès, Dolce & Gabbana, Gucci, and the rest of the most prized luxury brands of the era. Navigating the potential minefields of strong personalities with even stronger egos led to changes in strategy that resulted in unimaginable growth for many designers – and heartbreak for others. I learned that the rich, and the way they shop, are truly different.

In 2008, at the behest of my friend Angela Ahrendts – then CEO of Burberry – I took on my greatest challenge: London called; more specifically, Liberty of London, the world-renowned shopping landmark in London's West End and an iconic British institution. The board realized they would need a dynamic and fresh approach to recapture their lustre in London's rapidly evolving retail scene. Leading the planning of a broad renaissance for the store, we incorporated all aspects of the business and departments in the building. We doubled emerging departments and shrank or eliminated others, adding a variety of new and exciting product lines, as well as services and amenities with a focus and an edit ever mindful of the different bases that comprised the Liberty customer of the future. So, while Eskandar became the must-have for our classic customer, Alexander Wang ignited the young, trend-led fashionistas. Collaborations with brands using the iconic Liberty prints were similarly democratic, from Manolo Blahnik to Nike, Hermès and Target; all of whom kept Liberty in the public eye and aided the turnaround.

But there was still to come one more huge surprise – the power of British television! One of the traditions I brought to England was the 'open see' day, where aspiring designers are invited to showcase their work to buyers in a day-long marathon. The first such event generated such a huge amount of publicity that BBC2 decided to build a show around the concept: *Britain's Next Big Thing*. Ratings and reviews were very solid for a first outing, and sales and traffic within the store rose immediately. Liberty was on a roll and this momentum led to a three-part *Liberty of London* documentary, broadcast – after six long months of filming – in December 2013. Thankfully, all the time spent on this project paid a massive dividend – Liberty notched another huge gain in sales and traffic over those holidays, and with respectable ratings, we were invited back for Season 2 in the autumn of 2014.

And as all of this ensued, I found a constant challenge and delight in adapting to a new culture, complete with a colourful cast of characters, and in applying an outsider's slant on contemporary British life.

CHAPTER 1

MOMENTS OF CLARITY AND THE BEGINNING

It's easy, in retrospect, to pick out the pivotal moments of your life – when the course of your journey irrevocably altered. It could be that luck suddenly stepped in, or serendipity reunited you with a friend or significant person. Maybe out of the blue a moment of clarity prompted a change in direction or switching of tack. Rarely, however, do we know what these moments mean at the time.

As I stepped onto the sales floor of a fragrance hall of the giant Macy's in Herald Square, New York City, instructed to douse customers in Chanel or Givenchy (both, if they couldn't get away in time), there were few clues of where it would all lead.

At that time, November 1984, I was a recovering junkie. I'd just emerged from rehab following my second overdose of heroin, and I had been staying in army barracks in Groton, Connecticut, with my sister and her two young children, before moving home to Crestwood to stay with my parents. It's fair to say that I was at one of the lowest points in my life.

We were descending into a gloomy winter. My body had been whittled down to a wiry shadow of itself, my eyes were gaunt, and fading hope was written across my face. I was lost. I knew I was done with drugs – that was the easy part – but now I needed to find a job. I had trained as an accountant at college but never practised. Besides, not even street vendors, let alone an accountancy office, would see me as a viable candidate. I applied for every vacancy going in Manhattan: busboy, shelf-stacker, temporary secretarial work, fast-food counters. Everyone took one look at me and said *no*. My last port of call was the slightly crumbling, but iconic, Macy's in New York City. Perhaps they were desperate – it was the run-up to the Christmas season, after all. They were hiring, and they agreed to see me. 'Santa's Grotto or Fragrance Hall' was the deadpan offer from the store manager, seated in a strip-lit office with stale brown carpet. It was an easy decision; I opted for the fragrance hall.

And so it began. Strangely, from that first pestering spritz, I knew immediately that I liked this business. I wanted to know more. I loved making sales, and quickly understood the seduction of retail: the process of hooking someone and drawing them in, telling them stories and asking them questions, before introducing them to something they couldn't live without. It's an underappreciated art. What's more, I was surrounded with beautiful counter boys. Every day, everyone had a different date for lunch, and pretty soon that was me, too. At last, I'd landed somewhere positive.

What followed Macy's – that strange twist of fate – has been an incredible journey. It started out as something I needed – a chance, a shot, and some direction. I'd spent years since graduating flailing around, partying and dancing, before my unravelling. Jobs had simply been a vehicle to me, a means to an end to affording a ticket to the dance floor of a New York club, but this was the first I had actually enjoyed.

I could not have foretold where that lowly job on the beauty floor would have led. It's blossomed into a career that has been – essentially – my making. One that propelled me to New York City – not this time as a party boy, but as vice president and general manager of Henri Bendel, and then senior vice president at Bergdorf Goodman. It's put me front and centre of the fashion and beauty world – circulating with the great and the good: the Bobbi Browns, Michael Kors, Diane von Furstenbergs and Angela Ahrendts – witnessing their early careers and their subsequent success. But also mentoring young brand founders and designers, such as Luella Bartley, Jonathan Saunders and Alice Temperley, all of whom I was the first to take a chance on in the US.

It's sent me to England on a wild ride of Waitrose supermarkets, rain, more rain, and planning restrictions, to restore to its former glory one of the country's most beloved historic retail gems, Liberty of London. Along the way – for better or worse – it has also plopped my face on British television screens with the BBC's documentary on the store, exposing our nooks, crannies, personalities, and the treasure trove that is Liberty of London to the world.

Today I live in a small, sleepy mews cottage in Marylebone. I walk to work every day. Much – no, scrap that – *everything* seems to have changed since accepting that fateful post in Connecticut. Though, on reflection, a few basic things remain the same. Throughout my life, from age seven onwards and even during my LSD-dropping weekends at college, I have swum competitively. I love the solitude and the calm that swimming brings, and I swim every weekend, without fail. While I've ditched hedonism, I still love life – and I still love a glass, or two, of Pinot Noir with a cigarette of an evening (who am I kidding? Every evening). I still love to read, and to collect art. Most importantly, and what I am most proud of, is that the collection of friends, colleagues and contemporaries I have gathered along the way are still there, going right back to my early twenties pounding the shop floors of Bergdorf Goodman. In fact, Scott Tepper, one of my best friends from the Bergdorf Goodman era, and now reunited with me at Liberty, lives right next door to me in a cottage. Scott and I have known each other through thick and thin. We sit on the bench outside my cottage most evenings; we share a cigarette and marvel at how we got here – how we crossed the pond to this funny, brilliant country, where, despite the rain, people don't appear to own umbrellas, which they call 'brollies' (why?), while TV is the 'telly'. But I wouldn't change it. Not any of it.

* * *

At the time of writing, I am only fifty-six, but I feel like I've lived three or four different lives already.

I grew up thirty minutes outside New York, in a mid-sized town called Crestwood – in Yonkers, on the Bronx River, and built as part of the 1920s expansion of New York City. I have a sister, Beverly, who is five years older than me, and a brother, Jamie, who is five years younger.

My mother, Hannah, planned us apart like that, very precisely, so we'd be easy to manage, as she had contracted polio as a child, and suffered from health problems her whole life. One result of this planning, though, was that my siblings and I were never very close. In those critical, growing-up years, shared experiences foster intimacy between siblings – but we had none of that. We were like three satellites, each very independent, doing different things at different times, with little interest in each other. And so it remained for most of our lives. Only later did my sister and I really bond and, to this day, I am still learning what it is to be close with my brother.

My mother stayed at home to raise us. She was only ever able to walk at a slow pace and at times even had to carry around a small lightweight folding chair – she'd need to take a rest after every few paces.

Unfortunately, my mother couldn't plan for everything – my sister was a total rebel, a real handful. Beverly was always being picked up or kicked out of school for one thing or another. She got banned from high school for dyeing her hair in the toilets, and left home when she was just seventeen. As a child, I remember a dog biting her. Instead of running to my mother crying, she simply bit the dog back. That was her all over.

My brother Jamie, five years younger, was a stubborn homebody. Being much younger, he was of no interest to me or my sister, and he was also the most conventional, academic and 'straight' of the three of us. Jamie was interested in team sports and hanging out with his friends. My mother's youngest child, he really tested her energy for discipline, too.

Every meal was a battleground. My mother, never the skilled chef, fully embraced the newly fashionable convenience foods of the seventies. Every dinner was a reiteration of 'Helper Meal' (the food brand specializing in pasta sauces and meals, sold by General Mills under the Betty Crocker brand) – each one equally bland and laden with chemical additives. We were raised on that stuff. I have no idea how we ended up so healthy. Jamie refused to eat his ready meals and would sit, lips sealed, in a standoff at every meal. They eventually called a truce! He now works in finance and has a beautiful family.

By comparison, I was the quiet observer. I watched as Beverly created the drama – waiting until my twenties to stage my own rebellion.

My parents were very much a unit, a pair, and we were the distractions. My mother, Hannah, from German and Austrian parents, had grown up for the most part in Europe, outside Frankfurt, before settling in the US after the war. My father, Edwin, was a New Yorker through and through, and grew up in the neighbouring town.

My mother was always glamorous. She had brown hair, wore big black sunglasses and headscarves, and took huge pride in how she dressed. She had incredible style. She was also really smart, though she wasn't highly educated. She also had the uncanniest knack for impersonations, and could do someone perfectly after only five minutes of meeting them.

My father was average in looks – he looks a little like me – average height and demeanour, a strong nose and brown hair. He was completely devoted to my mother, and remained so right up until she passed away in January 2014.

My father had a small locksmith business in the next town. He was a fourth-generation locksmith, though that line ended with me, as did the family name Edwin: I am the last Edwin Burstell. I never knew until much later that he couldn't stand that little business – I had wondered why he never made us work there, but I think that was why; he just couldn't bear to subject us to it.

In the 1960s, he and my mother bought in to the promise of the Republican Party, believing hook, line and sinker that the party had their best interests at heart, and over the course of our lives I watched as what started out as a middle-class income, remained static, until it dwindled in the changing economy. Perhaps that's why Dad was forever escaping into a book, whenever he got the chance.

It was strange to watch, though. As I grew up, my friends left the neighbourhood, and bought nice new things. We, by contrast, stuck to vacations on the North Fork of Long Island, staying in small cabins and taking fishing trips with the working-class Greeks of New York. We would stay at a small resort owned by the Mott family. We'd go out and fish by day, then eat our catch at night. Again, each of us would remain highly separate. Beverly would seek out boys, invariably. I'd sail. Jamie would stay close to my mother or hit the playground.

The North Fork, back then, was the less upmarket side of Long Island – just like Brooklyn, I see it's being gentrified now, but back then it was where the poorer families vacationed. Everything about it was less picturesque than the glamorous southern fork. The sea was rougher, the beach was pebbly rather than sandy. Even the water seemed different – it was cold, treacherous and deep. There was a section of sea with a buoy that kids could swim out to, but there were frequent scares over the shoals of jellyfish that would descend on the beach, leaving children screaming and running terrified.

Our other vacation favourite was the Catskill Mountains. We'd pile into Dad's old 1957 Nomad station wagon and drive up to the mountains to visit the enormous wildlife centre. Or we'd visit Wildwood, the fairground town on the coast of New Jersey, with its boardwalks, rides, and cookie-cutter pastel motels, pools, parking lots and drive-ins.

Our family cars were always fraught with disaster and likely to break down at any point, which I found an adventure in itself. I'll always remember the Black Rambler we had at one point – its exhaust would pump out blossoming clouds of acrid black smoke wherever it went.

Back at home there was never much to do. This was the time of small shopping centres, before the tide of retail franchise homogeneity had descended on America: towns had their own establishments, rather than being plastered with freeways dotted in identikit Dunkin' Donuts, Taco Bells and McDonald's. These shopping centres were precursors to department stores, family-owned businesses that sold just about everything from fish hooks to freezer food and deckchairs, with relentless tannoy broadcasts offering 'specials'. Ours was called Klein's. There was also Gimble's, Altman's and Abraham & Strauss.

I worked at Finast, a local supermarket, stacking shelves to get by. I even faked my work papers to start there before the legal age of sixteen, but it still wasn't enough to go to a prestigious university – I ended up taking out a loan and studying accountancy at a local college with the help of my parents. Accountancy was the last thing I wanted to do but I had to do something, and if my parents were going to help, I had to pick something 'sensible'.

Looking back, it would be easy to apply some construct to this, to say that it unwittingly instilled in me some sense of entrepreneurial ambition, or that my father's modest income made me determined to make it big in business. But I wouldn't say it really did, not consciously anyway – and if it did, it took a good few years to manifest! I had a distinct period of being off the rails before I found my direction. It made me determined to escape Crestwood.

Even as a young child, I found life in Crestwood quite dull.

Everything about it was unremarkable. There were shopping centres, schools and parks – I always knew there had to be something more. The only thrill I got was from swimming. From the age of six onwards, I'd live for the whistle and crowds, jumping off the ledge and gliding into the cool, chlorine-laden pool water as the sounds of cheering muffled and bubbled, interspersed with bursts of sound as I turned and gasped for air. I still have the newspaper clippings with pictures of my small little body, an unrecognizable boy shivering in a bathing suit and clutching medals.

My family had an eclectic set of values: some refreshingly alternative, some stoically and typically conservative of the era. My father was Catholic and my mother was Lutheran (the same thing, but with less guilt), and yet both my parents supported abortion rights and were quite liberal in their thinking. My mother believed in alternative therapies – homeopathic and otherwise – which was quite rare for the time. I still have a great photograph of her eight months' pregnant with me, clutching a cigarette and a glass of wine. Those were the days! I 'came out' to them in my teenage years and they were unfazed. They were also, remarkably for the time, vegetarian for most of their lives. Most families were advocates of the steak-and-potato approach to life. Somehow, we never bought in to meat as a signifier of wealth and American Dream success. They just never saw the appeal. Maybe it was my mother's German heritage. She demonstrated a unique independence in her outlook on all things. Or maybe, it was that meat was too expensive. Either way, it rarely factored in our diets.

It was this spirit of open-mindedness that led my mother to agree to me visiting my Aunt Hedi in Europe every summer from the age of ten – my first escape from Crestwood, and the first in a series of formative twists that would change my life for ever.

My visits to my aunt began as an informal truce between my mother and her after they hadn't spoken for years – my aunt wanted one, or all of us, to go and stay with her in Frankfurt to cement relations, and I was volunteered as the symbolic dove of peace.

My aunt was different to my mother in every conceivable way; she was a little less glamorous but a bit more fearless. She had a different physicality: she was slightly more unkempt, heavier set, less made-up. And she was resolutely unapologetic.

Aunt Hedi had stayed in a small town, Konigstein, outside Frankfurt, Germany, to manage the family business while my mother moved to the US, but her mentality was anything but suburban. Visiting her was more like staying with Auntie Mame. She was single, frequently had live-in boyfriends, and was freewheeling and feisty.

Even before my first trip, there were early signs of a bond between us. We were kindred spirits. We'd exchange breathless letters, planning what to do over the break. I would treasure those letters; I couldn't wait to see the flash of the classic 'Air Mail / Par Avion' featherweight envelope – pale blue, with a border of red and navy blue chevrons. Then I'd arrive, we would pile our bags in the car and hit the road to any number of countries. Spain? Yes! France? Why not! It was incredibly liberating.

Every summer was an adventure.

What began as a caregiver-child dynamic evolved into an ironclad friendship. Aunt Hedi opened my eyes to the world, to life and adventure, and by the end of my teenage years we were more like friends. Years later, after all my debacles, I went to see her in hospital when she was suffering from Alzheimer's. To this day, it is my biggest regret that I missed the opportunity to say how much she meant to me while she was still alert. I was the last relative to see her in hospital. The stench of the ward hit me like a ton of bricks as I arrived and saw her lying there, a shadow of herself, staring into space. She didn't recognize me.

In the seventies, air travel was not what it is now. For starters, you couldn't fly direct to Germany from the US. I had to go to London first, then on to Frankfurt. During the Baader-Meinhof bombings of the seventies and eighties, we had to undergo full strip searches behind a curtain in order to board the plane. Scanners hadn't yet been invented. It was also a remarkable trait of that time that parents would allow a ten-year-old to travel on their own to Europe. Kids these days aren't even allowed to venture a few unaccompanied yards from their parents.

I remember my first trip. My mother and father took me to the airport and a freak storm ravaged the airfield; out of nowhere, the angry rain clouds formed, circling above the building. We were told there would be a delay, but my parents had left my brother and sister at home. They decided to leave me in the care of a soldier – people did that sort of thing then! The flight wound up being cancelled and so the airline put us on a bus to New York to stay in a hotel. Aged ten, I stayed a night in Manhattan with the soldier as my room-mate. Meanwhile, the soldier I'd been entrusted to went out for the evening and, curiously, never returned. I still think my parents never realized that this happened. I never knew what happened to that soldier either. I just remember cautiously picking up the phone in my room in the dingy 42nd Street hotel, The Commodore above Grand Central Station, and being asked to come down to the bus. This was before 42nd Street had been cleaned up, too. Every strip joint and porno theatre was still there – it was the seediest area in Manhattan.

It didn't get much better when I eventually arrived in Frankfurt. My aunt had not shown up to collect me. In shorts and a T-shirt, I sat on my little suitcase for hours, looking out at the tiled floors as throngs arrived, passed through, and left.

Time rolled on. I guessed she'd forgotten, but she eventually arrived – swinging around the collection point in her Audi, boyfriend and dog in tow and, crucially, without a care in the world. Off we went.

From then on, the world was our oyster. Germany was our home base each summer, but we never stayed for long. To this day, I find it inspiring that my aunt didn't care what people thought of her. She thumbed her nose at everybody. But at the same time I wondered if she was lonely. The relatives she had around her were old. She was tied to that little town because her income came from renting out the family bakery building. In retrospect, I think we offered each other an escape from the humdrum. I was her conduit to adventures, and she was my escape from Crestwood.

I would save up during the year to shop in Europe. Even then, European shops were something else. I loved shopping from an early age. On our trips I would buy trinkets and knick-knacks to decorate my room. By the end of my teens my room was covered in hand-carved candles, plaques and maps I'd collected. Who knew that all these years later I'd still love collecting junk – only it's more expensive junk now. I also loved European style. I couldn't afford the clothes, but I would take great inspiration from the beautiful cashmere sweaters, sleek-cut pants and crisp shirts, and would carefully weed out the closest cheap versions from the local Chess King store.

When I stayed at Hedi's we had a blast. I remember lazy summer afternoons making 'Drunken Peaches' when I was eleven: very early on, my aunt introduced me to the wonders of libation. Drunken Peaches involve putting a fresh, peeled peach into a chubby glass, pouring champagne over it, stabbing the peach flesh, drinking the champagne, then eating the peach. It was magical. I loved the first whisper of orange pigment as you stabbed the peach, and the tingling fizz of the cold bubbles lingering on the peach flesh when you bit into it. These cocktails were a daily ritual. By the time I turned twelve, we'd spend afternoons on the 'Hash Vista', smoking weed and looking out over Frankfurt.

For us, then, it was never 'just' drinking, or smoking, for sheer hedonism. That was not the point. It was just, well, what we did. I remember feeling buzzed, and this calm euphoria only added to the joy of escaping from boring old home. It never seemed dangerous, but little did I know that much later on all those demons would come back to me in an extreme, and altogether more frightening, way.

My Aunt Hedi, for her part, saw herself as my guide – the Virgil to my Dante – into adulthood. She loved to show me new things and thrust me into new exhilarating experiences.

On one memorable trip when I was fourteen, we went to Hamburg's infamous Reeperbahn, where all the prostitutes, strip bars and sex museums in the city are located. The Reeperbahn is sometimes also known as 'die sündigste Meile', or 'the most sinful mile'. Back then, it boasted Europe's biggest brothel, Eros, which was set over six floors. Hidden behind gates at either end, it was a strip-lit mecca for sex – a seventies Las Vegas of titillation. There were shop windows everywhere, with small doors through which people disappeared. It was funny, I never thought about it at the time but it was quite progressive to have a street like that. The authorities knew that prostitution went on, so they made a space for it to happen. Trust the Germans to organize sex! The old advertising adage of 'putting the goods in the window' springs to mind. Even now, when I see a woman wearing a sexy dress, I joke that she's put the goods in the window. I also apply it, of course, to the theatrical window displays of whichever store I manage.

I had no idea where I'd landed when we got there, but my Aunt Hedi had clearly decided that it was time for me to have my first sexual experience. She and her boyfriend left me with instructions to find them later.

I remember stepping beyond the gates. It was such a strange scenario: the music, the lights, the blasting noise. But I was more excited than scared. There were men and women in every window, some in dominatrix outfits, some naked. I found myself fascinated by the women's bodies as much as the men. It was pure sensory overload.

I walked down the street, from one thing to the next, before turning a corner to see the entrance for the Eros Centre, which occupied a dark underground car park off the main drag. There were a series of poles, on top of which there was a single light bulb shedding a column of light down on the body of a man or woman. All were calling out pick-up lines, compliments, and seductive invitations. Voices from the dark.

One good-looking young man started talking to me, coaxing me. I must have looked so scared and young in my shorts, ankle socks and button-up shirt! But I remember him being very reassuring, carefully picking out a selection of notes from the crumpled cash I shoved at him nervously. He led me into a small cabin where there was a hypnotic waft of incense, all the while speaking seductively in German. I had no idea what he was saying. Afterwards, I was quite shell-shocked, but exhilarated. It all felt very natural. The transparency of the street lent it legitimacy, somehow. Though when I emerged I was definitely ready to meet my aunt. The noise, the crowds, the colours, which had been exciting, seemed a bit blurry and overwhelming after that, and I quickly left the sexual fun pier to go back to the hotel.

I held on to the moment for a long time. It was three years before I would have what one could describe as even a casual boyfriend, so I thought about it every day. I was always sure about my sexuality, but there were still a huge number of questions at that time. Was I alone in my sexual orientation? Could I have a normal life? Being gay then was not like it is now. There was no internet, for one. At school you were quite instinctively aware of who else was, or wasn't, gay, but it was still quite unspoken. You still had to negotiate corridors of jocks and school bullies looking for any sign of deviance from the standard template of straight young American. Books became my gateway. I read a huge amount and eventually by reading various novels I became aware of San Francisco as 'it' – the mythic counter-cultural mecca, where homosexuality was normalized.

When a small clutch of high-school gay boys and I did discuss our sexuality, we talked about escaping to San Francisco. Though later on, when I got my driver's licence, I discovered that I didn't need to go to San Francisco, or even to Germany in fact, to have a gay sexual experience. I could drive thirty minutes up the road to an establishment. 'We' weren't all gathered on two streets on opposite sides of the coast. We were everywhere!

Other memories in Europe were more terrifying than fun. We were in Munich at the 1972 Olympics when eleven members of the Israeli Olympic team were killed after being taken hostage. To this day, it is one of the most disturbing experiences of my life.

It was September and the Olympics were in their second week. The day began with celebrations and pealing laughter everywhere. We'd been staying in a barn just outside Munich from which we travelled into town. Only we could choose a room where animals literally passed by us in the morning. No room at the inn! It was just like the nativity, only with Riesling.

At the stadium, I just remember staring at the blank monitors when the news got out that they'd been shot. There were no longer any scores. There was no information. Everything went eerily silent. It was like a vacuum suddenly sucked all the energy out of the place. Everyone knew something dreadful had happened.

We were so close to the massacre. I found it difficult to breathe. The experience had a profound effect on me. At that time, as an American, all conflicts took place on foreign soil. Here I was brought face-to-face with it. My aunt very quickly insisted we pack up and leave. I remember driving away, feeling that I could not come back from this moment.

***

Going home to Crestwood at the end of those summers spent with my aunt was always a 'thud' moment for me. Driving to the airport, my nose was a touch sun-kissed, I was a little taller (I still enjoyed regular growth spurts), and I was filled with memories of laughing on the road. The prospect of the long journey home filled me with despair.

The only thing I could ever think about during school semesters was when I would next visit Europe. Though, strangely, I was also mature enough to know it wasn't 'real'. My aunt at one point actually asked my mother to keep me. She wanted to send me to the international school in Frankfurt. My mother left the decision to me and I actually, even to my own surprise, found myself saying no. It was just too scary. It was as if a part of me knew that I needed the balance of a disciplined maternal figure, and that if I were fully exposed to life with my aunt it would be too much. Plus, I loved my family, even if Crestwood was stifling.

The only summer I took off from seeing my aunt was in 1974, when I got my driving licence. I took my driving test the second I was able to, and bought a red Volkswagen Fastback with savings I'd gathered from odd jobs. The car was beaten up, but it didn't matter. I loved it. It was a symbol of freedom – *my* freedom – from the crushing monotony of life in Crestwood.

I decided to visit Chicago and my sister Beverly, who by then was living with a hippy: a tall wiry man with hair down to his waist who was a bit of a drifter (people seemed able to drift back then, in a way they couldn't now. I never knew exactly what he did). The mission was made at the behest of my mother, again seeking to bridge the family divide by sending me as her dove of peace.

In the mid-seventies, I sported my own seventies look, with full bell-bottoms, giant suede platforms, long hair, and tight-fitting T-shirts. God, the seventies were bad in so many ways! And there was no escape . . . I spent a heady summer working odd jobs in Chicago with my sister sporting that very look. It was tough to wear flares well – harder than people realize. The jeans, even for men, were so tight that you needed a coat hanger to pull them up and you had to zip them up while lying down. For men, it also meant staying remarkably slim. The tightness meant they were very revealing, too – which was great if you were well endowed, but not so much if you weren't.

Up till that point, my sister had been estranged from the family. As she was five years older than me, we'd never spent that much time together, even when I was at home. I was the annoying kid brother, not a confidante. Which is why, in retrospect, I am so glad I made that trip. I arrived at the beginning of the summer, and by the end of it we were friends. I soon came to see that she wasn't so bad, even though she was a major rebel. She, like me, just couldn't take Crestwood. She was also bisexual, something I only learned when I visited her and she confided in me. It reassured me about my own sexuality. She had a boyfriend at the time, but had slept with women and was very open about it. That summer, after a day spent smoking joints and soaking up the sunshine, I told her I was gay and to my relief, she shrugged: 'So what? And?' It probably didn't mean much to her at the time, but that singular, casual response had a big impact on me and gave me a lot more confidence.

I was well established in high school at this point. When I returned from Chicago, I started to party with friends on weekends, either visiting the town gay bar or going to Manhattan. My parents always knew I was gay. I came out to them soon after I told my sister. They were more concerned about drugs.

I just managed to escape their gaze when I went to Iona College in New Rochelle, New York, twenty minutes up the road from Crestwood. In comparison to Crestwood, New Rochelle was a metropolis – it was bigger, growing, and had much more on offer. I started an accountancy course, moved in with two female room-mates, and the fun truly began. We would go out, party and go to bars.

I couldn't stand studying accountancy. I could add and subtract and do the debits and credits, but I just wanted the whole thing to be over. The only thing that kept me sane was taking a minor in English and living with those girls.

It was a mixture of frustration, impatience and boredom that made me increasingly experiment with drugs at this time. I found myself taking stronger and stronger types, from hash to pure THC, though I still kept myself together – Quaaludes, I found, balanced out the highs quite nicely. I regarded it as a weekend escape to cope with the monotony of accountancy. I wasn't dependent, testing the boundaries, or whatever other clichés could be applied. I just liked it and did it.

I was at college for four years. This was just when I also became more confident in my sexuality. I'd meet men in the local bar and date. Manhattan – notably Christopher Street in the West Village – was just a train ride away. I felt like if I couldn't get to San Francisco then I sure as hell was going to hang out in New York! Back then, the seventies, the gay scene in New York was all about Christopher Street. They used to call it the 'Wild, Wild West' at the time – and with good reason. It was so exciting. Christopher Street was the fulcrum of gay New York. It had been the heart of the Stonewall riots, which took their name from the Stonewall Inn on Christopher Street. In the seventies it was a twenty-four-hour party, with gay bars and fetish stores.

At last the end of my accountancy course arrived – not a moment too soon. It marked a strange turning point for me, though. I was relieved to finish my accountancy course but was by no means ready to join the real world. I'd been locked into the humdrum for four years and wanted to delay work for a bit.

So it transpired that Florida, hot with promise of beaches and boys, was the answer – a perfect escape from adulthood. What started out as a short segue, turned into a full year of debauchery, lost hours, sex and fun in Florida's beach party capital. And I wasn't done, even after that . . .

CHAPTER 2

LOST IN PARTY: ESCAPE TO FLORIDA AND NEW YORK, EXHILARATION, EMERGENCY ROOMS AND WAKING UP

'Hello,' growled a faintly familiar voice, a lower version of the American actor and playwright Harvey Fierstein's. 'Hello, Eddddd. It's Danny. It's me. I'm in England now. I saw you on the television.' It was 2012, a weekend in London. I'd been at Liberty for about two years and had come in, as I often do, to work on a Saturday morning.

At weekends, Liberty's tills ring on the shop floors and crowds throng outside, but the back-of-house offices during this time are defined by silence, the kind of vacuum-ish silence you only get from places that are usually filled with people and energy.

I'd dumped my stuff on my chair. The light was grey outside, and when I looked down I saw a red flashing beacon on my machine. I pressed it automatically, shuffling files, before his voice rang out.

There was Danny, my first true best friend – the bronzed boy I'd met on the first day of arriving in Fort Lauderdale, Florida, on my grand escape from adulthood.

Of course, his voice had descended by several octaves. It was a gravelly double bass after years of smoking cigarettes and doing God-knows-what. But he was still Danny, the chestnut-haired, good-looking boy who'd been my partner in crime all those years ago, clubbing, and lounging on the beach, laughing all the way at our good fortune (or not).

To experience Fort Lauderdale in the late seventies was to experience a unique period in time and gay cultural history, in the same way that early eighties Fire Island, New York, is still iconic to many for its beach houses, and legendary parties hosted by New York's gay glitterati.

Clustered along the Florida coastline north of Miami, 1920s pastel guest houses were being joined by the rapid development of giant gleaming condos – both attracted hordes of wealthy middle-aged gay men, along with hordes of party boys to entertain them, drawn by the heat, the white sand, the pulsating, hedonistic club scene and limitless eye candy.

Being openly gay in America at this point was still taboo, unless you lived in New York's West Village or San Francisco. Campness and flamboyance was reserved for the relative safety of Christopher Street. Yet here, in this slightly cheesy enclave of Florida, was an out-and-out gay village, a hotbed of decadent bath houses – where steam was the last thing on the menu, unless it involved a hot boy, or two – and where nightclubs were theatrical disco heavens.

Completing my degree in accountancy was a strange time for me. I was elated to have finally finished the thing and to have appeased my parents with a respectable professional qualification. But work, and joining the rat race or setting up a small business like my father's tiny locksmith's, was the last thing on my agenda.

My school friend Billy (who I'd known since grammar school) and I wanted to go somewhere hot to delay the onslaught of real life, and after a quick discussion, decided Fort Lauderdale would be our destination of choice. We reassured our parents that it would be a quick summer break. It turned out to be anything but.

We packed his beaten-up old Volkswagen Bug and drifted out of Crestwood with sunshine and beaches on our mind. It was going swimmingly, as we glided through state after state – Pennsylvania, then Virginia, then North Carolina – with crackly disco music pumping from the ancient radio and sodas from gas stations along the way, until our first calamity. We broke down – in South Carolina.

Never before had I regarded Crestwood as liberal but against the backdrop of South Carolina, in the Deep South, it felt positively cosmopolitan. There we were, two young boys in tight T-shirts, a million miles from home and stuck. Even the air felt different in the backwaters of South Carolina – heavy, hot and threatening, with the nagging vicious hum of grasshoppers. We were interlopers caught in foreign territory.

We waited for help after calling from a phone box, as truck after truck with various toothless locals went past, before eventually a tow truck pulled up. We were fanning ourselves to stave off the stifling heat as Bonnie Pointer's 'Heaven Must Have Sent You' was blasting on the stereo, when the overall-clad redneck climbed out and stared at us with an uncertain look. No wonder, to him we must have looked like two aliens from another planet in our cut-off jeans and tight T-shirts. He also didn't understand our car. Volkswagen Bugs then had their engines in the trunk, not the front. He opened the hood and was bewildered.

I remember thinking: 'This is it. We're going to die here!' He attached our car to his truck with a rope, silently, and we piled in the front seat of his truck, driving past ramshackle houses adorned in Confederate flags, until we reached the nearest town. We had to spend two days in that place while Billy's car was fixed. I didn't leave the motel room for the entire time.

To have this reaction, and indeed to remember this scenario so clearly now, may seem over the top, but these were different times and the South was a different place. Even now it isn't all that hospitable to gay men, but back then it was illegal to be homosexual in most states.

Suffice to say, we did make it out of there alive. I remember us eventually pulling on to the Fort Lauderdale Beach Boulevard at midday – the main strip of bars overlooking the beach, lined with bars and cafes and condo buildings – and already the scene was in full swing. The sun beat down. Smooth-chested, tanned boys were *everywhere*. Music was playing in every bar, while boys played volleyball.

My eyes bulged at this pastel-hued heaven with turquoise sea, palm trees and white sand. Why hadn't I discovered it sooner?

We managed to find a room at the Wish You Were Here Inn, a few blocks from the beach. It was one of the many rundown, small, deco, pastel-pink palaces, a relic of the 1920s Florida boom, which had been left to crumble as flashy condos took over (this was before these deco gems were reclaimed by hot hotelier Chris Blackwell, who bought up half of Miami Beach in the late 1990s).

Nothing was cool about the Wish You Were Here Inn, but it was cheap, and that's all that mattered. Billy and I quickly acclimatized. I grew a moustache, pronto.

Sunbathing was a serious business in Fort Lauderdale, attacked with systematic precision by all men. Every day began with sun worship. The beach was awash with bronzed gay men, there to see and be seen. Maintaining a body beautiful was also therefore a priority – achieved with many pull-ups and press-ups, and dancing to disco in clubs. The geography of sunbathing was paramount. If you weren't in front of the Marlin Beach Hotel on South Atlantic Boulevard you may as well be dead, which is why many of us (after only an hour's sleep from clubbing) would drag ourselves as early as possible to the beach to secure a prime tanning spot every day, popping a Quaalude on the way so we could sleep some more on the sun loungers.

The uniform back then in Fort Lauderdale was tank tops and Lycra – not a sleeve in sight. My skin quickly turned a deep nut-brown thanks to daily dedicated sessions in the sun, flipping on to my front and back at regular intervals, coated in a thick layer of Hawaiian Tropic scented oil. This was zero SPF sun care, needless to say. In any case, what did I care about aging? I was young.

We also took quite a creative approach to fashion. And by that, I mean getting crafty with the scissors. Those T-shirts didn't get fringes on their own, you know! We'd hack at T-shirts to create a new outfit every day, cutting off sleeves, cropping at the chest, allowing the edges to curl up into hems. We'd often turn to each other before going out clubbing and the exchange would go something like: 'What are you wearing tonight?' 'I don't know, what are you wearing tonight? Got a pair of scissors?' and then we'd create a new outfit.

Tea dances were a ritual. I've always thought the term 'tea dance' was rather funny – it conjures up images of British women in floral day dresses, sipping tea from cups and saucers and nibbling on cucumber sandwiches. Our tea dances were anything but genteel. They were drinks parties, held from 4 p.m. onwards with loud music and cocktail-hour prices. Essentially, they were like an early version of the afternoon ticketed clubbing events staged in Las

Vegas around hotel pools that they call 'day clubs'. Wall-to-wall flesh, booze, loud music and pools in the afternoon, they kicked off what daily segued neatly to twenty-four-hour dance sessions.

I met Danny on the first day I arrived. Billy and I had checked into the Wish You Were Here Inn, abandoned our bags, and hit the beach for our first tea dance. There he was, wearing a cropped T-shirt with 'Hot to Trot' emblazoned upon it, short shorts and sunglasses, sipping a cocktail with an umbrella in it.

He said he was from Long Island, and even had the classic Long Island accent. We'd both escaped the same humdrum of convention – in Danny's case, quite a difficult upbringing because his father had been very sick since he was a teenager. We both shared a wry sense of humour. We got along, because in spite of the fact that we bickered constantly, we saw a lot of ourselves in each other. After a few quips it was clear I'd found my tour guide and we remained inseparable for the duration of my time in Florida. People soon dubbed us Alice and Trixie after the hit US show *The Honeymooners*. It's now thirty years later and he still makes me laugh with stories of our misdemeanours – though his memory is better than mine.

To party with Danny was to dive, head first, into anything and everything, and see where you end up. We would frequently hit the clubs together. Danny had a job as a cocktail waiter at the Copa, the most popular club in Fort Lauderdale, so we were able to cut the line there and pretty much everywhere thanks to his connections. At the time the club staff uniform was blue and white striped Lycra short shorts. Waiters either had to go topless or wear a skimpy string vest on top, and flirt to within an inch of their lives. Needless to say, Danny, who was young and very pretty at that time, was rarely lonely. He was frequently groped by suitors who, in turn, were fought off by the bouncer he was seeing: a gruff, muscly, Tom of Finland figure.

Drag acts were a mainstay at the clubs in Florida back then. One of the frequent performers at the Copa was Belle Kinkaid, a six foot tall, formidable African-American drag queen specializing in Grace Jones. She used to have a very dramatic act that involved being lowered from the ceiling while singing. I remember once the rope snapped and she fell midway through, breaking her ankle. Even while the stretcher was carrying her away she was the consummate professional, lip-syncing to the final chorus of her song.

I had one rather wild, but hilarious, overnight liaison with Belle Kinkaid. I'll leave the contents of the evening to your imagination (for everyone's good), but it was worth it for the ultimate trophy – I made off the next day with Belle's Copa staff T-shirt.

Belle wasn't the only drag queen on the scene then. Divine was also a regular. I remember in the crowd one night, Danny and I shouted at her to perform 'Native New Yorker'. She didn't like the heckling too much. The first response down the crackly booming microphone was: 'Oh, shut up and shit on your face.' I'm still not clear exactly what it means but I remember us being such fans of hers we glossed over the insult and were simply over the moon she'd acknowledged us!

Danny loved being the centre of the party, which meant he was more creative in his dress than me. The Copa used to run Turnabout Nights, in which everyone was expected to cross-dress, and he used to dress up as Connie Francis, from the cult 1960 movie about Florida, *Where the Boys Are*. He also became so obsessed with a pair of red cowboy boots that he wore them even though they were a size too small for him. To date, I have no idea how he managed a night dancing with those things on, but he loved them, so that was that.

Danny and I, for all our bitching about our pedestrian home lives, did benefit from similarly open-minded parents. Mine had been very understanding about my sexuality when I told them. Danny's mother Audrey, a feisty broad if ever I saw one, was equally unfazed when he eventually confessed. He told her around this time he was confused as to whether he liked men or women and she retorted: 'What's there to be confused about? You are who you are and I love you whatever side of the fence you fall on. You could have the best of both worlds. But know this: if I ever catch you in my favourite heels, dresses or makeup, I'll break your legs.' How wonderful! That was Audrey. She used to smoke joints with us sometimes, too.

The clubs were a riot in Fort Lauderdale – cheesy, pastel, theatrical, and rammed to the rafters. One of my favourite bars was set underneath a swimming pool in a club called Backstreet. One side was made of glass so you could see swimmers diving in and frolicking; it was like an aquarium of beautiful boys in Speedos.

Backstreet was in downtown Fort Lauderdale and was designed like a playful Western saloon, with giant spinning fairground wooden carousel horses suspended over the DJ booth, and cowboy murals everywhere. Outside there were terraces, a jacuzzi and a pool with X-rated locker rooms, if you dared!

The main hotspot, though, was the legendary Copa, on South Federal Highway. It was dance heaven – turquoise outside, with neon lighting and white palm trees inside and a huge dance floor. Crowds lined the block to get in every night. There were a series of themed bars inside, including a separate one called the Pirates'

Cove, decked out in distressed wood, where porn played on loop on a monitor. Outside, on a big terrace, there were tiki bars.

Every night there were performers and drag acts playing and good-looking service staff – Madonna played there in its heyday (Madonna, not the world-famous 'Madonna' she is now, was a fixture on both the Florida and New York club scene at the time). Most nights I ended up in one or many of these places, before hitting the after-parties and crawling in at 6 a.m.

Looking back, the theatre of clubbing both in Florida at that time, and later in New York, had a profound impact on me. The parties were immersive, playful, themed and tongue-in-cheek. New York would soon experience a tidal wave of creativity in which acting, conceptual art and clubbing would converge with great groundbreaking venues attracting emerging artists, singers and performers. There's nothing like that now. There were simply no rules. When I'm thinking up a retail concept, or a window, and wondering if I've gone too far, I'll often think back to those disco balls and wooden horses and think, 'Nah, let's go for it!'

But back to Florida.

The Wish You Were Here Inn was a community in itself. I shared a room with Billy and two others, though they interchanged frequently, like a constant conveyor belt of escapees from suburbia. It was seedy and quite depressing, but we didn't care; we barely spent any time there and when we were, we were sleeping off the party so barely conscious of the cockroaches and tired drapes. For the whole time I was there I can't remember eating one single meal. Not one.

Fort Lauderdale was filled with boys like us, drifters drawn by the hot weather, cheap living, and safety in numbers that living alongside thousands of other gay men bought, and skimming off free drinks from the older, wealthier gay residents willing to pay for a flirt.

It may sound glamorous with all the parties, the discos and so on, but we were all very much living hand-to-mouth. We had to be quite scrappy to sustain that responsibility-free existence. We'd do odd jobs here and there, the bare minimum we needed to get by. The shallowness of the scene also got depressing. Yes, you could go out whenever you wanted and find an orgy of sex and drugs with strangers, but oddly, the more you did this, the less fulfilling it became. The best nights I had were out with friends, having drinks and dancing to disco for hours.

Can you have too much of a good thing? I thought not at first, but it did get draining after a while. Yet after almost a year there, I wasn't sure how to get out of it. Returning home wasn't a favourable option; I'd lost touch with my aunt and we'd sort of drifted. I didn't end up leaving Florida until I was flat broke and it became unbearable. Danny was still in love with the scene, so, with that, I said goodbye to him, and returned to Crestwood.

Danny and I stayed in touch for years afterwards but our lives took different paths. He remained in Florida for some time. When his father died in the early eighties, and I was back in New York, I drove straight back to Long Island for the funeral. Then he relocated to Philadelphia. These were his darkest years. He managed one of the biggest gay clubs in Philadelphia in his thirties, when he threw himself headlong into another non-stop party for several years. His body was less able to handle it; none of us could handle it at that age. I went to see him during this time for one crazy night at the club, indulging in all manner of substances, and had palpitations on the train back to New York. Soon after that visit, Danny returned to

Florida to clean up his act. Later on, we also became estranged (to my shame, during a significant break-up, I had skipped his fortieth birthday party). That 2012 voicemail in my London office was the first I'd heard from him in twelve years.

My parents didn't know what to make of me when I stepped out of the car outside their house on my return from Florida. Their son, a trained accountant and responsible adult, was rake thin, mahogany tanned, vacant and distracted. I got a local office job and couldn't bear the banality of life away from the sunshine coast. The partying may have been too much, but this stifling boredom was hell.

So, in search of more distractions, I started spending regular weekends in New York. Some of my friends from Fort Lauderdale, I found, had recently migrated to the city. They were getting serious about their careers, and hosting regular parties in their townhouses. I attended the soirees, gleeful for escape, and was gratified that they were still just as bacchanalian as Florida, with orgies, drink and music, but just a little more sophisticated this time – that is, better clothes and glassware.

It was this time that I met my first boyfriend, José, a muscle-bound Cuban financier. José was a fixture on the party scene and as a result I spent even more time in Manhattan with him. He was a true club boy, and introduced me to the most famous and notorious New York clubs of the time – which made the Florida club scene seem positively suburban. This was a party scene on steroids.

It was a relatively pragmatic partnership, and we split up amicably once it had run its course after a year. In fact, it was at some party or other after we'd split, that he'd introduced me to my new best friend, Dean.

First came heroin.

The disastrous effects of heroin, and heroin addiction, are obvious and well known – and it certainly didn't do me any favours – but I can see now there's a reason why people get hooked. I was introduced to it at one of these parties as a new 'wonder drug', and pretty soon was taking it regularly. It is a high like no other, almost indescribable; a very peaceful, blissful calm that takes over. You take one hit and you feel as placid as a lake, yet have a strange sense of clarity. From that first taste at the party, I was spellbound, and soon found I was habitually taking it alongside my portfolio of other vices. Soon I was shooting up daily.

Next came Dean.

I first encountered Dean at one of the limitless stream of New York cocktail parties in which people shout too much. He was ten years older than me, had incredible blue eyes, blond hair and pale skin, and was funny and irreverent. We immediately escaped whatever bash we were at for a night on the town. I stayed with him that night – though nothing happened, or would ever happen romantically – but we sealed our friendship for ever. Dean and I became fast friends and it wasn't much longer before I moved in.

Dean and I, like Danny and I, became inseparable right away and took to the club scene in Manhattan with dedication. I'm often asked why Dean and I didn't date. I think we considered it briefly, as Danny and I had, but quickly realized we were better as friends. Besides, I was seeing a very handsome man called Ricky, who lived on 115th and Madison Avenue in Spanish Harlem, and – despite the terrifying neighbourhood – brazened the streets daily sporting a bright purple Norma Kamali puffer jacket. The boy had some balls.

Dean and I lived in the West Village and rapidly slipped into a ritual of clubbing all night long. Rinse and repeat. We were out of control. We lived together for about two years, culminating in me overdosing on a cocktail of heroin, cocaine and alcohol, not once, but twice (I needed a second try, it turned out), before it became clear we were actually better apart.

Looking back, I don't know how I made ends meet. Hustling for tips in Florida is one thing, but my part-time office job wouldn't have got me much. Life in general was simpler and cheaper then, especially if you were frugal. You didn't need the smartphone plans, Netflix subscriptions and cold-pressed vegetable juices of today. All our money was spent on going out.

Dean had quite a respectable job. He was a high-powered financier and often subsidized me, though this was paradoxical too. I still don't know how he managed to maintain the work and partying without burning out.

We had some fun, too. You haven't lived until you've woken up one morning to the sound of a garbage truck at 6 a.m. because you've passed out next to them. We frequently passed out next to the garbage cans, jolted into alertness by the buzz of a stench-filled vehicle next to our heads. Then we'd decide to go home or go for breakfast.

Alongside New York's club scene sat Fire Island – an island off Long Island in New York and a popular gay weekend beach spot – and East Hampton. Dean and I would pile into a car on Thursday night and head to either one. Both had different scenes. The Hamptons was about big, posh money; Fire Island was just sleazy. It was more diverse, too. Parties were a free-for-all of all ages and all types who congregated in revelry at the houses of famous New York fashion designers.

I fell in love with Fire Island the first time I went. I loved the crowds and the parties. It was all about throngs of gorgeous people and parties. All the 'A-Gays' had houses in a row, neighbouring each other there, and people would skip between the two. The funniest thing was the mornings on the beach. After a big night, it was littered with bodies of people who'd passed out – like road kill, or giant sea lions on a Big Sur beach.

The Fire Island parties during this time were legendary. Every weekend one of the celebrities would have one. Here there were the regular themes – 'Think Pink!' – and alcohol and drugs on tap.

It was a strangely innocent type of hedonism in New York back then – particularly for gay men. Drugs, we knew, could harm us, but there were no sexual inhibitions at all, and we ran riot with it – with everything – exuberantly. Anything went. The clubs were sexual utopias, fantasy playgrounds to get lost in dance and surround oneself in a petting zoo of good-looking men.

This was the era of 'super gay clubs' – even grander and more theatrical than Florida, with sexual exploits even more extreme, both between the patrons and within the actual performances of sex on stage. A boa constrictor was once used in one of the acts at the Saint club, famously.

Dean and I spent every night at the Saint, in the East Village, Paradise Garage, 12 West or Area. Paradise Garage on King Street in SoHo had a huge scene (the logo famously featured a man kissing a tattoo on his bicep). Remarkably, it did not serve alcohol. This meant it could stay open all night, without legal restrictions, until the next morning. Many nightclubs exploited these loopholes, either not serving alcohol or giving it away free. Needless to say, it didn't really matter about the booze – these clubs were all about drugs, sex and dance.

The Saint, dubbed the first gay 'super' club, was vast – the scale was unimaginable. It could fit thousands of people, but was members only – you had to be endorsed by another member to get in. It opened in 1980 with a 5,000-square-foot dance floor covered by a huge planetarium dome, onto which they projected moving images. I remember my first time there – there were a thousand queens dancing and the projector gave one the impression that the sky was moving. Many of them toppled over because they were confused by the *trompe l'oeil*, combined with whatever hallucinogenic drug they'd taken. There were multiple floors, multiple bars. It was like nothing you could imagine. There was an upper balcony that overlooked the dance floor where men retired.

At many of the clubs, nudity or partial undress was normal and encouraged, so they had lockers to leave your clothes in. Or there'd be a theme, which required everyone to wear a costume, and several performances, such as ancient Rome, or 'All White'. Themes were big then, at both parties and clubs.

Running alongside this sonic gay clubbing scene in New York – a moustachioed army of buff boys – there was another alternative thread, an explosion of underground theatre and performance art, which Dean and I also loved. The East Village became the heart of this incredibly vibrant revolution – if you weren't seeing either some great piece of theatre or some horrible piece of theatre, you missed it.

There was a nightclub called the World, which converged the worlds of art, theatre, music and celebrity. It was set in a burnt-out block in the East Village with several floors that were theatrically dark, with scrappy walls and large balconies overlooking a dance floor. Rather than being like a regular dance club, there was an avant-garde fashion feel to this place – a bit like the hordes of theatrically dressed fashion students that attend London Fashion Week in the hope of being photographed. You thought about what you wore here and how to create a striking 'look' that was not only fashionable but also costumic.

Keith Haring, RuPaul, Stephen Sprouse and just about every other innovator club kid hung out in that place. John Kelly, the famous performance artist, also regularly appeared in clubs during this time. The Theatre of the Ridiculous, the underground avant-garde performance company founded in the 1960s, was big then, too. This group of performers epitomized the spirit of theatre at this time. They were creating performances on a shoestring and showing them for virtually no money. It was all about forging something new. This ethos remained thus throughout the eighties. Later, I'd go to shows with Quentin Crisp, the famed English writer and raconteur, and my then-boyfriend, Tom.

Grace Jones was a regular club performer. Her shows on New Year's Eve at 12 West were legendary. Funnily enough, years later she and I were on a flight from New York to London. She still looks incredible, and still has that brilliant booming voice. I remember hearing 'Give me some champagne!' in a husky baritone before seeing her enter the Upper Class area. You can take the girl out of the club, but you can't take the club out of the girl. She took a seat at the first-class bar alongside three gentlemen. Several hours later, and many champagnes later, she strutted off the plane in good shape. The three men (who had matched her drink for drink) had to be carried off by security . . . You don't survive Studio 54, and the New York eighties scene, without knowing how to handle your champagne.

In New York, the hub of the gay community in the seventies and early eighties was always Christopher Street. You couldn't drive a car down it on weekends. Crowds of gay men and women would throng around the bars, or onto the nearby piers, to party all night long. People wore outrageous outfits. It was a living, breathing catwalk, just like the scenes in the iconic documentary *Paris Is Burning*.

Later, at Henri Bendel, Bergdorf Goodman and Liberty of London, I'd visit real-life catwalks from Paris to London to New York, but those models – Kate Moss, Cara Delevingne, Naomi Campbell – have got nothing on the boys who paraded down Christopher Street and took part in the famous balls. Fashion was creative (designer, or you cobbled something together to make it look designer) and it was as much about the character, the facial expression, and arched eyebrow as anything else. Spectacular.

The Village's path to what it is now – one of the most expensive, gentrified, white, affluent neighbourhoods in Manhattan – very much mirrors how gay culture has evolved in the US. We moved in, made the Village beautiful, then people noticed and the prices shot up. So, we moved north to Chelsea and did the same thing. Then to Hell's Kitchen – though I am not sure *that* is quite beautiful yet!

But now we live everywhere. There are no specifically 'gay' neighbourhoods in New York, and that's because being gay has changed, thankfully. We don't – for the most part – need protection from the outside world, or to create our own enclaves. We are now openly the norm. We live everywhere.

***

The party in eighties New York on the gay club scene was seemingly unstoppable, until it stopped. In 1983, an article ran in

The New York Times that changed everything. They called it AIDS. Plop, the folded newspaper landed on every West Village and Haight-Ashbury doormat, Chernobyl-like in its effect on the gay communities.

A few articles had run before, describing a new, rare 'homosexual cancer', then this. I remember the headline: 'AIDS: A New Disease's Deadly Odyssey'. The reporter Robin Marantz Henig wrote the bad news:

> Medical detectives are calling it the century's most virulent epidemic. It is as relentless as leukemia, as contagious as hepatitis, and its cause has eluded researchers for more than two years. Acquired immune deficiency syndrome, or AIDS, was first seen in homosexual men – particularly those who were promiscuous – but it has now struck so many different groups that its course cannot be predicted . . .
>
> Half of the victims lived in New York City, and there was a large concentration of cases in California. Those studied were sexually promiscuous: Their average number of lifetime sexual contacts was 1,100; they frequented homosexual bars and bathhouses (where a typical visit may include sex with 15 to 20 deliberately anonymous men). Many of them also used 'poppers', inhalant amyl nitrite and butyl nitrite, drugs said to have the effect of enhancing orgasm.

Worse was that the outbreak unleashed a wave of open homophobia among popular pundits, who blamed the illness on our lifestyle, as some kind of divine punishment.

From the first big newspaper feature, a series of 'thud' moments made this strange enigma seem increasingly real, and tangible. A friend would die. A famous person in the gay community would mysteriously get sick and die of 'pneumonia' or for unexplained reasons (clearly, to us, from AIDS, which families often fought to cover up). Pretty soon AIDS had decimated the creative community in New York, and many of my friends – including, later, my most prized: Dean himself.

I remember he and I casually reading that *New York Times* article over breakfast. Of course, it was a shock, but our initial reaction was disbelief. The effect was instant, though. The gay club scene, which hinged on casual, unprotected sex, ground to a halt. And with it, many of those legendary venues were forced to close. Meanwhile, between 1984 and 1985, men began dying in their droves.

The first symptoms, among others, were losing a lot of weight. People got so, so thin. Then the famous lesions on the skin set in. Then, lesser known, it also caused blindness among sufferers.

The scariest thing was that it was so random. We'd all been doing the same stuff, but some men got it, and some didn't. It felt like a lottery. But that, in itself, affected your psyche. You lived with anticipation anxiety, examining any blemish, and cough or cold, with panicked horror. Because at that point getting it was a death sentence. We all started feverishly working out and beefing up our muscles to display health and vitality. This is strongly connected, in my view, to the big gym culture among gay men now.

Before long, there were so many men dying that many of us joined the Gay Men's Health Crisis (GMHC) to fight for better healthcare, more research and greater awareness, as the government and media had seemingly been ignoring us. The GMHC was driving the exploration of effective treatments and campaigning to release drugs.

I later supported the AIDS Coalition to Unleash Power, which launched in 1987. There was an increasing feeling of solidarity and anger among gay men throughout the eighties. In 1985 there was also the seminal play, *The Normal Heart*, written by Larry Kramer, a hugely emotive and powerful portrait of the crisis as it started in 1981, when men had first started dying and no one was talking about it. It was shown off-Broadway in 1985 and I remember being bowled over by the horror of it all, which had been so eloquently crystallized into a narrative. A lot of us were bowled over and mobilized to be more vocal as a result of this play. Radical protests were ramped up to get people's attention, from sit-ins to marches.

I managed to escape HIV and AIDS – a fact I am thankful for every day, because I certainly wasn't behaving responsibly enough to avoid it. But I was also testing my body in every way conceivable with drugs during this period.

I'd got into a cycle of being out every single night of the week, using speed to be up, downers to sleep, and in larger and larger quantities. The big drug then was cocaine to start an evening. Off you'd go with a blast, trot, trot, trot! But I was also taking heroin. Dean and I both loved to drink too, which was frequently calamitous. When you take cocaine your body revs up and you simply don't feel the effects of the alcohol you're drinking, or heroin to the same extent. Your body is processing everything so fast it tricks you into thinking you can handle more . . . But things, eventually, collide. You collapse and start sweating. At the same time, Dean and I were just getting more and more isolated. We found ourselves out of sync with the highness or drunkenness of people at the party, always being far worse; far higher, far lower. It was the beginning of the end.

At my most extreme, I was mainlining heroin daily. For me it had been progressive. I had simply got more and more used to it, and in combination with other drugs. I had to keep escalating the amount I took to feel anything. I would do it in the backs of cars, in restaurant bathrooms. Sometimes, your body would react unexpectedly and it would be a frightening experience – sometimes an out-of-body one. You'd be emptying a syringe into your arm and suddenly know you'd taken things a bit too far. You'd know it was happening; your mind would be racing with thoughts: 'Holy shit! I cooked a big one!' but you'd be powerless to do anything. Then your head would suddenly droop, thud, and you'd be out, with a needle still hanging from you.

Obtaining the gear was a challenge in itself – it often involved going to the bowels of Brooklyn, which was not the leafy hipster-fied enclave it is now. I remember many occasions waiting anxiously outside a dealer's house in a car, while a friend went inside, thinking that any moment I would be attacked. We'd shoot up in the car!

The other remarkable thing was that, while I was an extreme case, drug use was actually popular among many yuppies in New York. I was day-to-day, but there were plenty of weekend junkies out there, partying to extreme on the weekends and then holding down high-powered jobs in the week.

My parents didn't know about the first time I overdosed. I was taken to the Cabrini Medical Center, downtown. I remember waking, totally disoriented, and wondering where I was. It gave me a real shock. I vowed, of course, that I would calm down and never get myself in that situation again. But then, a few months later, it did happen again. This time much worse. It was at Dean's apartment. He discovered me and knew he had to get me out of the apartment – if I had died in his place, he might have been charged with murder. He left me, slipping in and out of consciousness, on the sidewalk and called my mum, who came with my aunt – who was staying at the time – to collect me. I had to spend a day at my parents' house – and then Beverly saved my life by getting me transferred to a rehab centre.

I was admitted to a psychiatric ward and strapped to a bed. They put me on constant observation for forty-eight hours because their theory is that you could do anything. I woke up, slowly, to those beige walls and starched sheets. When they unstrapped me, I tried to open the window but it only opened an inch.

Back then, drug addiction was lumped with every illness going, so my ward featured every kind of case. I remember, three days after I arrived, a guy was wheeled in on a bed next to me, his hands in fists facing up to the ceiling, rested on a pillow, with blood-sodden bandages from his slashed wrists. That moment, right then, was the lowest point in my life.

I had to stay in hospital for two months. The clinical smell, the constant squeak of sneakers on the floor, reinforced the inescapable, oppressive 'clunk' of it all. One of the worst things was that the drugs had affected my balance, so I had to have therapy to get that back. That, on top of endless group therapy, was exhausting but effective.

My parents were shell-shocked by the whole thing. I was more ashamed to see my Aunt Hedi, though. I can't forget her look of disappointment when she came to see me there.

Dean didn't come to see me in hospital. We spoke, of course, but there was an unspoken understanding that we should keep our distance for a while. We were still friends, though, right up until he died.

Eventually two months had passed and already I was getting this restless feeling. I'd woken up. Two months without so much as a sniff of a beer had clarified everything for me. I wanted to get started with my life. I'd wasted enough time.

I was signed out by the doctor and, after staying with my sister briefly, moved home where I applied for, and got, my job at Herald Square's Macy's. Who knew such a crummy holiday job could have such miraculous consequences?! It hauled me in the right direction.

Dean wasn't so lucky. He managed to continue partying for a while, but called me a year or so after we'd parted ways to tell me he'd got it. AIDS, that is.

It is one of the most devastating things in the world to watch a best friend die. Dean, for his part, fought it with everything he had. He tried meditation. He slept outdoors in freezing weather overnight as part of some crackpot therapy. He'd talk to angels. Later he wore an implant portal in his chest where he administered all sorts of drugs. That sort of thing was typical then – men were trying anything and everything in a desperate bid to stay alive.

Eventually, Dean went blind. In his bleakest moment he asked me for advice – not for new suggestions on medications, but on what combination of Class A drugs and alcohol I'd put together a few years back to make myself overdose. He simply wanted to end it. Pretty soon, he died naturally anyway.

Living with AIDS – AIDS full stop – was horrific. Walking around the Village you'd see men battling different stages. AIDS still is, of course, horrific, but in the early eighties it was new, unknown and terrifying. To get it was a death sentence. This is an era few gay men of a certain generation will ever forget, not least for the countless friends they lost during that time.

CHAPTER 3

A NEW START: MACY'S, LESSONS IN RETAIL, HIGHS AND HARD KNOCKS

I remember stepping on the shop floor at Macy's with some trepidation. This was my first job in several months, and the first one since I'd become clean. The lights all seemed impossibly bright and the crowds were frenetic. One day after another, sipping sugary black coffee from a paper cup in the alley outside the store, heaving in as many cigarettes as I could get through in fifteen minutes. I did get used to it, though, and before long I actually started to enjoy it.

Holiday music on repeat was comical but cheering. Plus, the scene was social, fun and uplifting. And I had purpose. Over the next few years my love of retail would grow from these early days into something I not only enjoyed, but was good at.

It's still staggering to me that from this point, starting as a spritzer boy in Macy's at Christmas, just over a decade later I'd be given the top job at one of New York's iconic stores, Henri Bendel, and later the jewel in its crown as senior vice president at Bergdorf Goodman. Not to say there wasn't blood, sweat, tears – more spritzes where that came from – and some serious beauty witches in between. But I made it.

Macy's Herald Square in the mid-eighties was a retail destination for every tourist, office worker and student. It was also a superhighway for commuters switching between Penn Station and the Herald Square subway in the morning: Macy's store occupied the block in between and many would use it as a shortcut. Commuters would charge through its vast beauty halls on the ground floor, zigzagging past the pillars and makeup stands every morning. It was frenetic for us store boys, but also quite amusing. There you were, trying to hook them in, and they were trying to dodge you, like football players in their white sneakers, tights and pencil skirts (very *Working Girl*), or trenches and shoulder-padded suits for the men.

Macy's sales staff was famed at the time, not just for their tenacity with a bottle of scent, but also for their good looks. On the beauty floor if you were nothing else, you had to be *hot* (not sure how I got in!). We were all approached on a daily basis by a variety of suitors from middle-aged men with comb-over hairstyles to attractive students from the nearby Fashion Institute of Technology (FIT).

The counters were circular in Macy's, set around pillars, so there'd be ten of us stood next to each other spritzing outward. We never dated each other – far too complicated – but we all, on some silly level, bought into that fantasy of a millionaire showing up one day and 'rescuing us from all this'. Or, being rescued by someone – *anyone* – like puppies in the pound: 'My real parents finally found me!'

Selling fragrances in Macy's was remarkably easy. It was like shooting fish in a barrel, due to the pure volume of traffic. Though still, there were daily fights between sales clerks over who had made a sale, who had stolen a customer, or who was responsible for spritzing a customer in the eye.

At Macy's and later at Bloomingdale's, it became a frequent

occurrence for customers to try to sue the store as a result of a near-blinding by scent. But it was unavoidable sometimes. I remember in my early spritzing days, I hadn't mastered the directional spritz (the trick is to mist it just a few yards in front of a moving customer – the idea being they walk into a wonderful pouf of enticing scent). Estimate their walking speed wrong though, and this could be disastrous. You'd either get them in the ear, or the eye. Pretty soon, customers got wise to the opportunities too – in other words, as more successful law suits against retailers occurred from errant spritzing, some scam artist shoppers would stand deliberately in harm's way, then claim they'd been blinded.

Thankfully I have never been sued, but I did have some near misses at Macy's with a perfume bottle in hand. The best you can hope for is irritated bewilderment; the worst, tears and a call for your manager. Once, after one particularly misdirected 'pouf', a woman slapped me. It was winter, she was wrapped up in a fur coat and hat and had been stomping on the superhighway beauty floor with purpose. I saw her from afar and thought, 'This is it! My next sale!' only to misjudge one of her sudden weaves to dodge a customer, spraying the scent straight in her face. It was a knee-jerk response for her to slap me, and I think we were both as shocked as each other. I did a sharp intake of breath as the sting grew on my cheek – yes, she'd slapped me, but I was a lowly spritzer boy, and she was the customer. Thankfully, she quickly apologized and bought the scent. Another drama averted.

It was a 101 in selling though. You quickly learned how to flatter, when to flirt, when not to, and how to convert someone who was simply browsing into someone walking away with a bottle of Paco Rabanne.

The scents were very heavy back then. If a fragrance was sweet, it was cloyingly sweet. If it was spicy, it was incredibly spicy. The campaigns, too, were overt. I remember Yves Saint Laurent's Kouros, launched first in 1981, being huge – advertised by a muscle-bound torso of a man. There was no room for subtlety.

In the run-up to Christmas you couldn't walk through the department without your clothes becoming saturated in scent. It was a crazy time for workers, too. We opened every night until midnight in the run-up to Christmas Eve, when we were due to be closed at 7 p.m. I remember it got to 6.55 p.m. on Christmas Eve the year I was there. We were supposed to be processing the final transactions before the doors shut. Despite this, the counters were still five people deep with desperate shoppers clutching armfuls of products.

The bell rang to signal the store closing – like a school bell ringing in freedom – and instead of wrapping up the last transactions, all the staff who'd been working twelve-hour shifts for weeks let out a spontaneous whoop. It was over. Everyone ditched their counter or shelf-stacking and practically ran to the lockers to fetch their bags, leaving dumbfounded and outraged shoppers stranded with their goods, unable to pay. We didn't care. We were on vacation – for a day, at least.

Despite the rivalry for commission, there was a funny sense of camaraderie at Macy's. We'd each punch our card in the morning on the old punching machines, 'phump!' and punch out, 'phump!' (Yes, they still had those machines. The 'phumpers', I liked to call them.) We'd punch each other's cards as a favour sometimes, even though this was a sackable offence. We'd also rescue each other from the unwanted, creepy advances of customers.

It was a revealing introduction to retail theatre. Macy's beauty floor was so bright, beaming and sparkly, it looked like a spaceship in the middle of Manhattan. But there was a reason all the boys looked so great: they were impeccably lit. In spring, they ramped the theatrics up even further, with a garden theme, decking out the whole place wall-to-wall with plants, birds and foliage, complete with squawking soundtrack on repeat. It was all grandeur. If only the customers saw the tattered lockers, scuffed corners and beige walls behind the scenes.

I held out at Macy's for six months, through the squawking of the garden theme, and through countless bottles of Kouros, before starting to get restless. My commission rate proved I had a knack for selling, but I wanted to move beyond being a mere spritzer boy. I also wanted to earn some more money so that I could escape my parents' house; the final straw was my brother getting a fancy finance job. I needed to catch up. Fast. Neiman Marcus in Westchester was advertising for sales assistants on the beauty floor and I applied.

Neiman Marcus at that time was the shopping hub for Westchester's wealthy residents – a giant store with the angular modern frontage and the company's signature handwritten lettering emblazoned on the side. Newly opened, it was one of the latest in a wave of luxury department stores, from Nordstrom to Bloomingdale's, which had started opening regional suburban outposts from the seventies onwards, taking advantage of affluent suburbanites.

In the early eighties, with the flourishing US economy, Westchester was riding high. The clientele at Neiman Marcus were predominantly executive wives who'd flocked to the nearby suburbs with their families, but still wanted their piece of luxury, and had cosmopolitan tastes from the formative years they'd spent in the city. It was a world away from the scrum at Macy's. The products were better and priced higher. Naturally, the clientele had more money too. All of which spelled one very alluring thing to me: better commission.

As a sales assistant I was placed higher in the ranking than a lowly spritzer. I could cover the entire department and all the brands, taking one customer through all their needs from Chanel to La Prairie. I had to sell differently for this new type of consumer. Everything about selling to the sophisticated local Neiman's women required a slower and more conversational approach; not to mention empathy, which I fabricated from the ether: 'Oh, I know. It is *so* hard to get a great summer clutch mid-season . . .'

I also had to learn about the beauty world quickly. Spritzing is one thing, but selling to this customer meant understanding the USP, the ingredients and benefit of buying every product and brand stocked on the beauty floor, which back then was everything. It meant understanding beauty regimens and being able to put together a tailor-made package for customers, understanding their different needs. 'T-zone? Pores?' The beauty world back then, as now, had concocted a plethora of ailments and imperfections to mask with new magic products.

Alarmingly, part of my role was also to administer occasional makeovers, a fact which still amuses my staff at Liberty of London. I was given some training for this – mercifully for the women of Westchester – but my early attempts were more drag queen than suburban goddess. But, somehow, I got it down. Before long I was applying eye shadow with the best of them, which all contributed to a rapidly rising sales record.

I also met Tom Beebe at this point, the head of visual merchandising at the store, who became my partner for the next eighteen years. Though this didn't start so well. I ran into him on one of my first days, stood at the top of a ladder in a store window fixing decorations, wearing big headphones and singing 1982 disco hit 'Gloria' by Laura Branigan out of tune. To this day I can hear the atonal 'Gloria!' blasts he shouted. I remember thinking: 'Who is this wiry, tone-deaf man?' We didn't like each other at first, but we became friends after a while and then dated. He's very funny, has a lot of energy and, despite the fact we're like chalk and cheese, there's an ease between us. Even now, when we get together we're like two old shoes.

Another meeting at Neiman Marcus would have a big impact on my career, and land me with another lifetime friend. Sharon Collier joined Neiman Marcus as my manager on the same day I joined. She had just relocated from Dallas, Texas, due to her husband's new job in New York City running Borghese cosmetics. I still remember her walking onto the shop floor. She was ten years older than me and exuded bold Texan glamour. She was pale and tall and slim, with big blonde hair and a gentle Lone Star lilt in her voice. She'd relocated with her husband but was far from a housewife. Sharon was ambitious, and very quickly started making changes in the department, with hopes of rising through the ranks, if not of Neiman Marcus, then of another store. She also took a shine to me, encouraging me after a short while to move into beauty buying.

Sharon was firm with me from the beginning. Working on, and managing, the sales floor is vital to understanding the customers and consumer behaviour. It's a great foundation in retail and can be highly lucrative – some love it and stay doing it for ever – but if you want new challenges and to climb the ranks, you need to build on this and enter retail buying or management. This was a language I understood. My brother was a high-flyer in finance and I was already aware that I was behind in my career, thanks to all my escapades. Plus, I loved the idea of buying. I was good at selling. What could be so hard? I mentally hitched my wagon to hers, learning the ropes as fast as I could.

It was easy to admire Sharon. She had a relaxed manner, but was also extremely quick. She'd see a department and immediately know what was needed to turn it around. I think she saw a kindred spirit in me. Then, Neiman Marcus could be quite dour and I think she liked that I was enthusiastic about her ideas and trying new things. She was looking for a partner, someone to support her in this, and thankfully she picked me for the part.

A few months passed and suddenly Sharon announced she'd been given a job co-directing the beauty floor buying at Bonwit Teller, the illustrious (but then slightly ailing) gem of a New York department store in Manhattan. I was devastated at first, thinking she'd deserted me in Westchester, but it turned out it was just the opposite. An assistant beauty buyer job came up and she quickly poached me. I remember it coinciding with me winning an Employee of the Month award at Neiman Marcus. I got it for my sales record one day, and the next day turned on my heel: 'I'm going to the City to work with Sharon!' (Well, not quite as dramatic as this. But you get the picture.)

It was perfect timing. I'd been desperate to move out of my parents' place and Tom and I, by then quite serious, decided to get a flat together in the City. Tom was soon promoted to head of merchandising for the East Coast US, and would spend the next few years using New York as a base to visit Boston, Florida, and all the other East Coast stores.

This was also a significant marker in terms of my turnaround. By this point, I'd got fully immersed in the business of retail on the ground level and was thriving on making sales and succeeding at something. I was also, perversely, thriving on the routine. I'd finally decided to grow up.

Bonwit Teller & Co. is one of New York City's iconic historical department stores which, in its 1950s heyday, was on a par with Bergdorf Goodman and Saks Fifth Avenue as the place to be seen for wealthy women. Founded in 1897, it was another of the esteemed Fifth Avenue stores dedicated to serving New York's carriage trade, but by the early eighties, its star was fading as its rivals blossomed. (Carriage trade is the rather old-fashioned term given to old moneyed consumers. It was coined in the early 1900s, describing people who could still afford to keep a private horse and carriage.)

Bonwit Teller & Co. had occupied the corner of Fifth Avenue and 57th street, a beautiful art deco New York landmark (and former Stewart & Co. building) since the 1930s but throughout the decades after had endured – as they so often did – a series of buyouts and management changes. In 1980 it had also lost its flagship, when the landmark was sold to Donald Trump and demolished to build Trump Tower. The new Bonwit Teller & Co. store was attached to the new Trump Tower mall and was significantly smaller than the original.

Poor Bonwit Teller & Co. You can still catch glimpses of the Fifth Avenue original deco store if you watch 1961's *Breakfast at Tiffany's* as Audrey Hepburn's taxi pulls up past it to arrive at Tiffany & Co., but that is all that's left of the beautiful building. I still remember its incredible big windows. It was one of the glorious emporiums of its time.

I joined Bonwit Teller & Co. in 1985, when the company was still alive but on a downward trajectory, mainly because it had been slow to keep up to date with the rapidly moving New York retail scene (Bergdorf Goodman had a similar audience but had somehow managed to transition, keeping its carriage trade but also attracting new customers). It still had a few good years left at this stage though, and a prestigious reputation as a retail Grande Dame. We had our work cut out for its beauty halls but Sharon and I were excited to update it by introducing some new beauty brands.

This was my training ground for beauty buying: I learned volumes from the experience. You see, negotiating isn't really an art if it's from a position of strength. If you are in a position of strength, like I was later at Bloomingdale's, there's no skill involved, because you can bark orders until you get what you want.

If you're negotiating from a position of weakness, you have to be more creative, get inside the head of your vendor, and find other ways to broker a deal with them. If you can't give them a massive order on one thing, perhaps you can add value in another segment, and so on. I learned all of this at Bonwit Teller & Co., sat at a cramped desk with four other assistant buyers. I still remember chain-smoking with them in the office while hitting the phones between appointments. We smoked like chimneys, operating in a constant grey fog, taking it in turns to clean out the bucket-size tray of dead cigarette ash at the end of the day. Yuk! I hasten to add that I have since cut down on the smoking and reassigned the spare disposable funds to Pinot Noir.

There were other lessons besides negotiations. One tough day I learned a harsh one, when a senior buyer told me I wasn't able to come on appointments with a big-name vendor because I wasn't properly dressed. I remember being absolutely devastated, before looking down, regarding my skinny jeans, sneakers, thrift-store denim shirt and skinny tie and wondering if she had a point. She put it as nicely as she could. Well, not really: 'There's no way you're coming to meet Estée Lauder with me if you're dressed like that. This is Estée Lauder.' But I rolled with the punches, smartened up, and went shopping.

My haphazard way of dressing, and style, would follow me throughout my career, with frequent makeovers and new wardrobes. This occasion marked the first. Bloomingdale's marked my ascent to Armani and all things shoulder-padded. Meanwhile, Bergdorf Goodman would teach me in the art of pocket squares and starched collars.

My offices, too, would turn out to be a far cry from the slick environs of retail giants such as Marvin Traub of Bloomingdale's, or the cream and salmon minimalism of Bergdorf Goodman's Dawn Mello in their time. Though these I have never changed.

My offices are a bit like me. They're mini mind-collages, with photographs on the wall, clippings of magazine pages I find inspirational, knick-knacks I've collected on my travels, stacks of coffee-table books I love and, of course, overpriced scented candles. (The *New York Post*, which once ran a feature on famous retail offices, described mine at Henri Bendel as 'a little off the wall'. Ha!). I've also evolved a uniform of sorts at Liberty of London, somewhere between smart and quirky, much like the store.

Tom's and my taste in apartments was similar – he always had an eye for a great place because his job was so visual. He also had an incredible collection of furniture and art. We were endlessly moving and finding new environments to put a stamp on. Tom could make a pile of shit look fabulous, wherever we were, and was great at reinventing and reclaiming household items and fashioning them into fabulous design objects. I've learned all my interior tricks from him. I still try and knock-off his style in my own apartments now – though am rarely as successful.

In our time together we lived in various locations downtown in New York. Our first place was in Gramercy Park. We lasted there a year. We then moved to 16th Street in the original Chelsea Hotel. Then Fifth Avenue, when no one was on lower Fifth Avenue. Then we finally ended up on West 11th Street, in a historic townhouse off Bleecker Street. Tom transformed this space – so much so that it got photographed in *New York Magazine*'s interiors section. He'd cleverly created new floor lamps using 1950s shades, commissioning new stands. Our art lined the walls. He'd also used actual white picket fencing to create a wall decoration in the bedroom – which sounds bizarre but, trust me, it worked. It was very witty.

I've continued in this vein ever since – the impatient relocating, that is. I can't stay in one apartment for longer than a year before I start scouting out other areas and buildings, planning out my new ideal home.

***

Sharon and I worked well together at Bonwit Teller & Co. and we quickly managed to score a couple of successes, which led to rising sales in beauty. We managed to get some new brands, and it all seemed to be heading in the right direction. We had a good two years together there, before Sharon made the leap to Calvin Klein and I made the daunting jump to the beauty fast lane: Bloomingdale's.

The rule at Bloomingdale's is that you have to be a beauty floor manager there for at least a year, whatever your experience, before you can be a buyer. At the time, Bloomingdale's was the hottest store in New York, the meeting place where rich Upper East Side kids flocked to spend their weekends socializing, and nowhere was more densely populated than the beauty floor on ground level.

Beauty was experiencing massive growth at this time, as hordes of affluent young professional women in the city had started splurging on premium beauty indulgences for themselves. The past couple of decades had seen an explosion in colour makeup, skincare and fragrances and the big expansion of beauty giants Estée Lauder, Lancôme, Chanel and Elizabeth Arden. Beauty floors were accounting for a larger and larger chunk of retail store profits, and so had become prime commercial real estate. In 1986, a Barnard's Retail Marketing Report estimated that cosmetics averaged sales of $350 a square foot, compared with between $80 and $120 a square foot for clothing – a huge difference.

I'd wanted to move to Bloomingdale's for some time. It really was the epicentre of retail in Manhattan at that point and so, with some trepidation, in 1985 I accepted the job as a beauty floor manager, even though that was a slight demotion. I eventually made it to buyer though, surviving five years of the torture, but escaped to Henri Bendel when I'd learned everything I needed to – and not a second longer.

To be that big and successful you had to be slick, and that is what the Bloomingdale's beauty department was. There were four hundred beauty sales associates at Bloomingdale's and the beauty floor spanned 25,400 square feet. It was a well-oiled machine of young sales assistants, each expert in the art of clinching the deal with a sale, even if it meant being cut-throat. It was a constant revolving door which I had to referee, making sure each fragrance launch got maximum sales for the brand, that there weren't any fights, and that the buying team were happy.

It was about two days into this job that I realized what I had let myself in for. On a weekly basis I'd be at war with the buying team. Meanwhile, on a daily basis I'd be breaking up fights between sales assistants (or found gently weeping in a restroom stall). 'Who gets the commercial TV?' 'Who stole my model?' 'Someone stole my sign!' It was a constant battle. Though, of course, amid the maddening ambient music, twinkly lights and manic grins on the shop floor, you'd never have known it, looking in.

At the time, Tom and I were living in a small apartment in Gramercy Park. He'd be flying around to various Neiman Marcus stores, or we'd be together in New York, sampling one of the endless merry-go-round of 'must-go-right-now' restaurants. New York in the eighties was all about restaurants, but not so much the food as the who, the what, and how to get a reservation. I seem to remember most of my lunch breaks in the eighties were spent on hold to the reservation line at Indochine, Gotham, Texarkana, Nell's or whichever other joint was creating buzz at the time. Indochine, in NoHo near Washington Square Park, is one of the most famous from that era. The legendary French-Vietnamese restaurant was a hotspot and the ultimate hangout scene on weekends, populated by the who's who of New York from Anna Sui to Calvin Klein to Salman Rushdie, who'd eat then party. We'd often go and eat there, people-watch, then hit Tunnel (another legendary eighties hotspot, set in an old railroad freight terminal in Chelsea. It has since faded and was even the butt of a joke in *Sex and the City* as one of Carrie's early haunts). After that we'd wind up at Tiffany or Empire Diner for breakfast at 4 a.m.

It was also around this time we discovered Montauk. Not the Montauk you know now – Ibiza in the Hamptons. At that point Montauk, on the farthest point of Long Island, was remote, blustery, and populated only by a group of hardy locals. I loved the sense of isolation there. Nothing about it was trendy. It was a blue-collar fishing town with no boutiques – just a few bars and hardware stores. We'd go for New Year and nothing would be open, except for perhaps the Shagwong, a spit-and-sawdust bar and seafood restaurant with a neon sign, red booths, plastic place mats and beer. Everyone in town went to the Shagwong. There was only one motel: the Memory Motel, a shabby establishment, which was an unlikely icon thanks to Mick Jagger, who wrote a song named after it after staying in Montauk in the seventies. By the eighties it had kept the shabby charm, but as a result of its rock-and-roll status had a relatively busy bar. We'd get in the car, throw on our flannel shirts (to blend in) and sip beers after a walk on the beach. We were part of a growing group of people in Montauk, including artists such as Peter Beard, Julian Schnabel, and Andy Warhol.

All this I fitted in around a seventy-hour week and stressful job. I am not sure how I did it even now.

My day at Bloomingdale's did finally arrive though. A buyer opportunity overseeing Estée Lauder came up and I went for it. Estée Lauder then accounted for a huge amount of business at Bloomingdale's – it had its own buyer overseeing it. It was a massive role, but I was determined that, after marshalling a fleet of sales assistants for over a year, I was going to get it.

As Estée Lauder was one of the most important vendors to

Bloomingdale's beauty floor, and Bloomingdale's overall, Marvin Traub, the CEO and president of the store, had taken a great interest in who got the job of managing the account. He wanted to make sure they weren't a boob – the stakes were high. This meant that each one of the managers had to go for a personal interview with him in his gigantic office. I remember going up to the executive floor, my palms sweaty with fear, before cautiously sitting down on his leather sofa. In walked Traub, a tall, stately man with soft eyes. He didn't sit at the desk, as I expected. Instead, he came and sat next to me, casually putting his feet on the table, before asking how I was.

In retrospect I think this was a tactic to get me to relax, or at least to be disarming. He was extremely nice, though, and a world away from the merciless behaviour of his staff. In retrospect I think this might have been the secret to Bloomingdale's success. He was the charm, letting the pack hounds of buyers fight underneath him. It's his incredible manner that secured amazing partnerships and beauty exclusives for Bloomingdale's, and made it what it was.

He had fantastic vision. Traub loved a spectacle, and understood its importance to retail. Each year, Bloomingdale's would host a themed promotion by country across the store, such as 'India, the Ultimate Fantasy' and 'China: Heralding the Dawn of the New Era'. These promotions were immersive with huge budgets and elaborate decorations, costumes for staff throughout, musical performances and themed boutiques. They'd import curated goods from the country in question and also invite famous designers to come up with themed pieces to sell.

It was equally theatrical for new store openings. During the seventies and eighties, Bloomingdale's was adding more regional stores, which had similarly extravagant launches. For its

Philadelphia King of Prussia Mall opening in the mid-eighties, a marching band played to waiting fans as a fleet of helicopters landed in the parking lot. Each contained a designer – Oscar de La Renta, Calvin Klein and Donna Karan – stepping out individually to arrive: an *Apocalypse Now* of fashion. For the company's launch in Willow Grove, also in Philadelphia, Traub organized a circus of jugglers, clowns and performers. Diane von Furstenberg rode in on the back of an elephant.

Traub has always been charming to me since. After I left Bloomingdale's, even right until his death, we kept in touch about various business projects. He kept working to the age of eighty-seven when he died (in 2012), which is remarkable. But that was him.

Suffice to say that on that first meeting with him, I got over my shock. We talked a bit before he cut to the chase: 'Are you tough?' he asked. 'Er, yes!' I answered back, my tone perhaps a little too nervous. I found out a few days later I got the job and was elated, but also terrified at what lay in store.

The management style at Bloomingdale's was to throw you against the ropes, again and again and again, until you figured it out. You either figured it out, or you left. That was that. I was shown to my new office on the buying floor, and introduced to the five other buyers on my team. There were two fragrance buyers, one for men, one for women, and then three buyers split the rest of cosmetics between them.

At the time we were led by two beauty heads: Gertrude and Jane (at least, that's what I'm calling them to protect their identities), the two pit masters, who were tough but talented and skilled negotiators. They would pitch all the buyers against each other to see who won. The store calendar had fifty-two weeks and each week the buyers had to fight it out for budget and real estate and a great location on the beauty floor to showcase a new product.

Our response was twofold. We did compete, naturally. Our job depended on it, after all. But we all knew we were in the trenches together, too. We'd come in each day and exchange glances thinking: 'Whose turn is it? What did they think up today?'

I met Heidi Manheimer on my first day on the job. We both started on the same day and she was the cosmetics buyer on the team. She had short, dark, pixie-cut hair and brown eyes, and was slim, with a wicked sense of humour. She had the office next to mine and we became thick as thieves. We'd walk home some days in stunned silence, in a total daze. Then we'd build each other back up.

We also developed a shorthand. For example, Heidi soon learned that my big night out was Thursdays (Friday nights are for amateurs). I'd go out clubbing all night with Tom and crawl into work with a pretzel, or some other heavy dough product, and try to survive the day. She would come in on Fridays and slam the door extra loud, exclaiming, 'Helloooo Ed! Hellooo! How are you?' I clearly forgave her as Heidi and I still speak once a week. Today she is the CEO of Shiseido Cosmetics America.

Heidi and I, together with the three other buyers, were responsible for the massive beauty department revenues at Bloomingdale's. Which, in reality, meant that every day something was our fault. If the sales were low, not only in New York but other Bloomingdale's branches, somehow it was our fault. If there was a snowstorm affecting sales, it was our fault. If there was a flood in the basement, it was our fault. And what if the stockroom workers hadn't brought up the products to the shop floor? Our fault. I learned to use a forklift truck during this time, to avoid a lashing by taking up goods myself – another secret skill for my list. Between makeovers and forklifts I have a few backup careers if retail goes down the pan.

Everything was about *sell, sell, sell* at Bloomingdale's. Buyers meetings would be an ordeal if you hadn't made target. The insults were direct, humiliating and harsh. It was five years of conflict, but it taught me everything about precisely the kind of management style not to support. I've never thought that blame culture or fear is a great motivator of people. Ever since I began managing people, I have actively sought to discourage it.

I let off steam at Bloomingdale's by clubbing on Thursdays or going to the theatre with Tom in the evenings. My weekend clothing style could not have been more different to my work style, which was buttoned-up Armani grey suiting. Come Thursday, I'd be wearing leggings and a big black Japanese tunic on Christopher Street.

It was around then that Tom and I started hanging out with Quentin Crisp. Our friendship with Quentin was unlikely to say the least. I used to read his pieces in the *New York Native*, a gay biweekly newspaper that was published in the eighties, and was a big fan. I said to Tom one day on a whim, 'I want to meet him! Let's call him!' This was in the days of the phone book and we managed to get his number fairly easily. He lived on East 3rd Street in a rooming house then, across from the notorious Hells Angels motorcycle club. We said we'd like to take him to lunch to a great place on Fifth Street I knew, and strangely enough, he accepted.

I remember us both sitting there bickering before his arrival. 'He's not coming, you idiot!' 'Yes he is! Shhh!' And then his figure appeared in the doorway. The lunch lasted long into the afternoon and from there we embarked on a ten-year friendship, until he died. He was as outspoken and eccentric as you'd imagine, with his faintly tinted purple hair swept atop his head and neckerchiefs always tied artfully around his neck.

It was a friendship that had a profound effect on me in retrospect. I admired Quentin for his pure chutzpah as a gay man. He was out and proud way before it was openly accepted, which can't have been easy. He also had fight in him, and kept working – like Marvin Traub – right until the end. It's remarkable that this man moved to New York in the late seventies and effectively started his life afresh aged seventy-two. He had a one-man stage show, wrote plays, and wrote columns. He was hugely active.

In person, he was fascinating and extremely witty but also had an endearing way of still getting excited about things – he loved it when I bought him eyeliner from Bloomingdale's for his birthday once. He was also friends with his scary neighbours the Hells Angels, who were infamous for once killing a man at a Rolling Stones concert when they were reportedly hired by the band to handle its security. Quentin and the Hells Angels got along just fine, somehow.

Despite being visibly successful, Quentin's apartment was about the size of a small closet. He always lived quite hand-to-mouth, which I don't think people realized. He also suffered terribly from psoriasis, the condition that causes red flaky skin. He kept covered up a lot as a result, but again, he never let it affect his conversation.

We went to the theatre most of the time, going to see everything from the *Glass Menagerie* to *Tommy*. It's funny, you look back at his reviews for the *New York Native* magazine and he always writes something like: 'I went to the theatre last night, with the visual king and his constant companion.' (Tom was the former, I the latter.) We, meanwhile, dubbed him 'QC'. He took great care of his appearance and always wore a hat, a jacket and scarf.

New Yorkers loved him but he was also an anomaly. He was incredibly opinionated, sometimes compromising his popularity. His views on gay marriage, for example, were quite polarizing in the gay community. His whole argument was: why would I want to assimilate? He also made derogatory comments about the royal family and marriage, which caused ripples of disapproval in the British press.

In many ways he was the ultimate outsider. He used to joke that he was a UFO, as somehow he'd managed to travel, rent, and work virtually without any papers. Though he, himself, was a big documentarist. He'd scribble frantically in his diary, which he called the 'Sacred Book', recording everything.

In his later years, towards the 1990s, Quentin's health started to decline. He had pneumonia among other ailments, but continued to work on regardless. He was very committed, so if a job had been booked in the diary, that was it. It was under such an obligation that he eventually died. He had been booked in the UK to do a revival of his one-man show and despite ailing health made the flight over. He died in his sleep the night before the opening. It was so surreal to read about it in the papers, our friend, but even in death I think he made a sly wink to us. We'd taken him to see a Charles Busch play years ago and our seats had been reserved with name cards. Quentin loved his so much – '*Reserved for Quentin Crisp*' – he took it home and hung it in his tiny one-room apartment. This sign was photographed in his *New York Times* obituary.

***

If the beauty world in the late eighties and early nineties was about any main category, it was fragrance. Fragrance after blockbuster fragrance was launching at this time. There was a high success but also a high flop rate. Everyone had a signature scent then – Liza Minnelli, Marlo Thomas, Cher, everybody. In 1985, forty-one fragrances, including Calvin Klein's Obsession, and Beautiful by Estée Lauder, launched globally. In 1991, fifteen fragrances launched in Bloomingdale's alone (often with an exclusive), while thirty others were discontinued in the same year. Fragrance had become the affordable indulgence for women, moving from an occasional gift to an everyday part of women's regimes. Meanwhile, fragrances had become the cash cow of every luxury brand. As Traub commented in his 1994 memoir: 'If a woman couldn't afford a Chanel suit or handbag, she would buy the fragrance. The more out-of-reach the image, the more successful the fragrance.'

Giorgio Beverly Hills' eponymous fragrance, Giorgio, was perhaps the biggest fragrance at this time (and of all time). It had launched prior to my arrival but was still doing huge business when I arrived at Bloomingdale's. Giorgio Beverly Hills was a famous boutique in Los Angeles launched in 1961 by Fred Hayman and George Grant on Rodeo Drive, known for its yellow and white striped awnings which later became synonymous with Beverly Hills, and boasted famous patrons including Princess Grace of Monaco, Natalie Wood and Elizabeth Taylor. In the late seventies they wanted to leverage all that Hollywood mystique, and in 1981 launched a fragrance in matching yellow and white striped packaging. At first they only sold it in their Rodeo Drive boutique, but then Bloomingdale's negotiated an exclusive on the launch in the East Coast when their public relations director Margot Rogoff discovered it on a trip to Los Angeles and thought it would be a hit with customers.

Something about Giorgio struck a chord with US consumers at the time. It symbolized all the joyful exuberance of luxury in the eighties – aspirational, bold-faced wealth, fused with the allure of Beverly Hills' manicured lawns, palm tree avenues and sunshine. It was a potent mixture, and pretty soon Giorgio was doing annual sales of $8 million at Bloomingdale's, and $60 million overall for the brand. It was a complete bonanza and an ongoing success for Bloomingdale's.

Giorgio was an overpowering fragrance. You could smell it coming from a mile off on the shop floor. It was potent, floral and heady. They'd give away towels and cardigans with it. To this day, if I catch a whiff, I am ready to vomit.

Fendi's launch was a major fanfare and continued to be a star product at Bloomingdale's after its 1985 launch. I remember the sales assistants were trained to wistfully exclaim 'The Passion of Rome!' as they spritzed unsuspecting customers. The launch of Fendi's fragrance at Bloomingdale's is now legendary. It was estimated to have cost $200,000. The five Fendi sisters flew in from Rome wearing fur coats. Every window was given over to the scent. Meanwhile, on the beauty floor was an aisle of giant Roman torsos.

Bloomingdale's was famed for its theatrical blockbuster fragrance launches. They even used to call the central aisle of the beauty department 'B-Way' (referencing Broadway, Beauty-Way and Bloomingdale's-Way simultaneously). It had a black and white chequerboard floor and a black ceiling. This was the stage set, and the real estate each buyer fought for when launching a product.

Bloomingdale's, for some time, had been famous for its spritzers.

Think of the cliché beauty department spritzing today and it all starts with Bloomingdale's. You couldn't get out of Bloomingdale's during this time without being attacked by some pouf of mist. It was a running joke. During the eighties, the store tripled the number of paid spritzers and they weren't limited to the cosmetics floor, either. They'd be in the designer departments, everywhere. As at Macy's, Bloomingdale's had been sued a few times for spritzing people in the eye. As a result, it became policy to ask customers if they'd like to be spritzed first but regardless, the atmospheric fog of floral notes worked its way into whatever everyone was wearing.

Though Bloomingdale's was a slick operation, the huge scale and speed of turnover, along with ever-ambitious theatrics, at times led to calamities. I remember when Elizabeth Arden launched a mousse foundation product when mousse was the all new exciting delivery method. To launch the mousse they dressed up two models in giant mousse-can costumes with only their faces pointing out of helmets. They were hilarious to look at – just like the giant foam burger and hotdog suits you get on out-of-work actors outside fast-food joints. I am not entirely sure how Elizabeth Arden thought these costumes would convey sophistication and aspiration, but one thing was for sure: they stood out. Only problem was, the mousse-can men were also blind as a result of their helmets.

I remember taking one look at them and knowing that it was a bad idea. Their instructions were to walk around the beauty department handing out samples but because of their limited vision they kept getting lost, hobbling like stray Duracell bunnies. Within five minutes of them being unleashed, my heart was having palpitations as they scattered and destroyed. I stood on tiptoe, looking out at the throngs of Bloomingdale's shoppers in the beauty department, as the metal cans blundered their way from display to display, knocking into customers here and there. But worse came when I couldn't see what was happening. Within minutes, the bumbling blind mousse cans had made their way onto different floors and into different departments by accident, knocking over hat displays, plates, you name it. Then came the complaints and tirades, all heightened by the usual day-to-day dramas on the beauty floor.

My recurring memory is getting calls, every minute, on the minute, from the homewear department to the candle department, complaining about the errant mousse cans. 'Er, Ed. Can you come and get the mousse cans out of here?' Then five minutes later: 'Hi Ed. We're in jewellery. Can you come and get the mousse cans?' It was that kind of wacky stuff every day.

Every now and again you get a new category of product that becomes a total phenomenon. My time at Bloomingdale's saw the launch of two significant ones: epilators and potpourri. Funnily enough, and thankfully, both crazes have abated in the meantime.

First came epilating. The Epilady was the first handheld device of its kind, promising perfect hair removal for women without the side effects of shaved legs. Two Israeli engineers had created it in 1985, with the intention of revolutionising hair removal. In Israel, 200,000 had been sold within the first year, so naturally we wanted it at Bloomingdale's. We launched the product and it was a total sensation.

Epiladies were sold as the saviour of womankind – ignoring the fact that they mechanically tear out multiple hairs, simultaneously, from the root, which was incredibly painful (current models are reportedly more gentle).

It was a huge success story in the American press. The problem? It hurt! It was a new torture device. We sold zillions at Bloomingdale's, but zillions came right back. I remember even Joan Rivers made a joke about walking down the street in New York and hearing women behind closed doors, unsure if they were being attacked or just epilating.

Then there was potpourri. It seems so ludicrous now – a bowl of coloured, scented woodchips with the odd acorn being the height of sophistication, but in the late eighties, potpourri was seen as a pure bag of joy (and a licence to print money for those who sold it).

Potpourri – so the story goes – started life in seventeenth-century France. The French preserved flowers and spices in pots with salts, which were then placed in containers with perforated lids to gently scent rooms. Fast-forward to seventies America and influential decorators had started reviving the practice, placing bowls of rosebuds, scented with botanical oils and herbs, around the interiors of new projects for their wealthy clients. Soon, in the late seventies, chic establishment stores like Henri Bendel had started carrying potpourri lines by brands like San Francisco-based home fragrance company Agraria.

By the eighties, potpourri had officially gone mainstream, and bananas. It was everywhere. The refined rosebuds had been adapted to include anything from cinnamon sticks and acorns to wood shavings. Manufacturers had also got creative with colourings – red, blue, sparkly white – anything went. In 1989, it's reported that potpourri sales were totalling $260 million. Every lounge, hotel room, office and restaurant had a bowl of the junk.

At Bloomingdale's, we couldn't get it on the shop floor quick enough, particularly in the holidays. Every time I replenished the table it was cleared by the baying mob of New Yorkers in search of an easy gift. I remember during this time having to use a wheelbarrow to transport enough to the beauty floor, and not even having time to stack packets. I ended up just tipping them into a mound on the table, like multi-coloured food into a trough, as hands grabbed desperately at them.

Who could stray from such career highs? Heidi and I stuck it out as long as we could but by the late eighties, after five years of indentured servitude, we were both plotting our exits. Heidi ended up jumping ship to Barneys to direct cosmetics buying. I had been interviewing anywhere I could, including applying for numerous roles at Bergdorf Goodman, but was eventually offered a role at Henri Bendel as beauty buyer. It was a smaller, *much* smaller, operation and role than Bloomingdale's, but Henri Bendel had recently been bought by The Limited Inc., which had plans to transform it into a brand. I took my chances and handed in my notice. My leaving send-off from Bloomingdale's was perhaps the swiftest and most gleeful in history. I left the bar with a 'Don't forget to write! Byeee!' and quickly set about trying to erase the mousse cans from my memory.

CHAPTER 4

THE BIG BREAK: HENRI BENDEL

I practically skipped to work on my first day in 1988 as beauty buyer at Henri Bendel. I was free at last from Bloomingdale's, and here was the opportunity to work in one of New York's truly iconic speciality stores and wave goodbye to the army of spritzers. The sun was shining and the coffee I'd bought was warm in my hands. Somehow, I felt there was a good omen about this move. Though I didn't realize then how spot-on my instincts were, not even close. Who could have known I'd be at Henri Bendel for over a decade and eventually run the joint?

I started out as beauty buyer at Henri Bendel, and over the course of the next fourteen years would be given department after department to oversee until, in the most miraculous twist of fate yet, I would be given the top job as general manager of the whole store. I'd work with retail icons Angela Ahrendts and Ted Marlow along the way. I'd also weather the storm from Henri Bendel's expansion to numerous locations across the US under The Limited Inc. back to a single store, and the launch, and subsequent shuttering, of a Henri Bendel luxury clothing brand.

Over the years, there would be heartbreak – a painful break up with Tom, my partner of eighteen years; a few subsequent affairs, and break-ups; and many, many reflective glasses of wine looking out onto the beach in Montauk. But major highs, too.

In many ways my time at Henri Bendel was my making. Necessity (or in some cases, calamity) turned out to be a true mother of invention, and saw me resort to a host of crazy stunts to bring Henri Bendel back from the brink. I also proved myself as a leader in retail. This transition solidified my ambition even further. I proved myself at Henri Bendel and found myself wanting to do so again, and again, at every level in retail until I got to the top of the food chain. Somehow, with the help of great mentors, great friends, and a sprinkling of 'Go big, or go home' bravado, I pulled it off.

Henri Bendel is a New York institution, famed for being the place where Manhattan's elite shops for cutting-edge high fashion. It has never been as big as players like Saks Fifth Avenue, or as fast-paced as Bloomingdale's, but that is the point – it has always been the authoritative secret haunt, a jewel box for the affluent few to find the latest looks for their cocktail parties.

Henri Bendel, the man, was a milliner by trade and set up a hat store which also sold imported dresses in Greenwich Village in 1895. From there, the business had blossomed into an influential luxury boutique for New York's wealthy – it was one of the earliest stockists of Coco Chanel. In the early 1900s, such was its growing success, it moved to a new, expansive location on 10 West 57th Street: a slim building with a large arched iron entrance, and vast windows on every floor. At the time, the area was residential but it soon became a vibrant shopping area, in which Henri Bendel thrived.

From the 1960s onwards, Henri Bendel had been edited

mercilessly – but shrewdly – by president Geraldine Stutz, one of the last true 'doyennes' of fashion, who had introduced Stephen Burrows, Perry Ellis, Jean Muir, Sonia Rykiel, Carlos Falchi, Mary McFadden, Holly Harp and Ralph Lauren among others. Like Browns boutique in London, Henri Bendel was famed for being the first to get any new label, mainly because of Geraldine Stutz.

Stutz was the figurehead of the store. Her most famous move was transforming the ground floor of Henri Bendel in 1958 into a theatre set 'Street of Shops'; a series of miniature boutiques, inspired by a buying trip to Europe. Each small 'shop' sold something different, from hats, to objets d'art, to gift-wrapping. Later, it had dedicated designer boutiques, such as Stephen Burrows' shop, which opened in 1969. The street was the talk of Manhattan, and the envy of all retailers for decades after. It is widely seen as the precursor to the modern shop-in-shop concept we have now. It also revived the then-ailing store, returning it to profit while establishing it as 'the' place to go for Manhattan's society women.

Stutz herself, a formidable and flamboyant character, embodied the store's mood – she was a fixture at fashion parties, often wearing a turban, or some other dramatic accessory. Her clothing taste for Henri Bendel was described as 'dog whistle fashion' because its focus was on 'clothes with a pitch so high and special that only the thinnest and most sophisticated woman could hear their call'. (The store was famous for stocking garments no larger than a size 2.)

By the mid-eighties, the store still enjoyed this reputation, but sales had slowed and it was in trouble. In stepped The Limited Inc., one of the US's biggest retail behemoths (and owners of Victoria's Secret), which bought the store in 1985.

The Limited Inc. was drawn to Henri Bendel's sleek image and wanted to grow the business into a global brand. It had plans to put Henri Bendels in every regional mall from Chicago to Dallas, while also launching a new Henri Bendel luxury brand. 'There is the potential for Bendel's in every major city of the world,' said the company's chairman at the time, Leslie Wexner, touting the company's bullish ambition to *Women's Wear Daily*.

The Limited Inc had bought Bendel with promises of working closely with Stutz, of course, and barely tweaking a window display. But relations soon deteriorated – as they so often do in this scenario – between the store's head and its new owners. Stutz left in 1986.

The Limited Inc. quickly went about transforming Henri Bendel. They started discontinuing unprofitable lines and departments. They introduced new automated payment systems and more accessible fashion labels. They also soon moved the store from its historic location to a new bigger building at 712 Fifth Avenue.

By the early 1990s, Henri Bendel was in the middle of this transition. No longer the beacon of sophistication it once was, but not yet the blockbuster commercial luxury business its owners were aiming for, it needed help.

I stepped into Henri Bendel at this time as a beauty buyer, two years before they moved into the new Fifth Avenue location. The fashion press, avid supporters of Stutz, were publicly mourning the 'death of Bendel's' – especially as many of its brands were in the process of defecting to Bergdorf Goodman.

When I got the offer from Henri Bendel, I'd been at Bloomingdale's for five years, doggedly fighting it out as a beauty buyer in the den of snakes, while interviewing wherever I could to escape. The pace, the bitchiness, the repetition of mega-brand after mega-brand creating identikit fanfare for fragrance launches, had driven me to the point of insanity, as had the backstabbing.

If Bloomingdale's does nothing else, it teaches you about the discipline of numbers. Numbers, numbers, numbers – though, frustratingly, this had done me no good in countless interviews at Bergdorf Goodman, where I was turned down many times for a job, I suspect because of my poorly cut suits! It was only when I later joined Bergdorf Goodman that I truly learned how to do Bergdorf polish.

My time at Bloomingdale's had also taught me about retail theatre, something that would come in handy much later when – with limited budgets – as general manager of Henri Bendel, I would try to put it back on the map.

In 1990 there was uncertainty about The Limited Inc.'s plans for Henri Bendel, but I saw it as an opportunity. Doubtless, The Limited Inc.'s approach to Henri Bendel was different, and I'm pretty sure Stutz would have been horrified at some of the spectacles I introduced (including naked men in bathtubs in the store windows!). But the upper crust, 'dog whistle', elitist approach to fashion was holding less and less currency in New York, and the audience was shrinking, giving way to a new, younger customer who wanted accessible fashion, and big bold names.

People didn't need to be told what fashion to wear any more either – they were increasingly confident in their choices, rather than prescribed 'trends', and didn't need the seal of approval from any store, or fashion doyenne, to guide them. This, for me, marked the beginning of the end for the tradition of having fashion director figureheads run stores.

There was a lucrative opportunity in reaching this new group of consumers and The Limited Inc. wanted to make damned sure Henri Bendel got them.

I signed on the dotted line, supported by Tom, and we embarked on our next adventure.

It was a fun time for me during these early years at Henri Bendel. I was full of optimism with my new job. Tom and I were established with our various apartments (we moved frequently, requiring constant redecorating) and loved life in the city. I'd become a collector of books – a habit I'd inherited from my father. I also become an avid collector of music. Even now, my friends mock my music collection. On any given trip to a store I will buy alt-J, rare disco albums, La Hell Gang – anything, and in batches of ten. I'm probably the only one who still buys CDs, and have been propping up the ailing record store business for the past twenty years. Tom and I filled our apartments with art, music, books and artifacts, and went out constantly.

We'd also travel together as much as we could, though vacations were often fraught with calamities (we were somehow prone to comedies of errors). I remember going to St Maarten in the Caribbean. I'd read about this incredible beach, and so we'd set off in our rental car determined to find it. All the signs in St Maarten are in French and Dutch, so we couldn't understand any of it, except the name of the beach. When we arrived at our destination, a police car was at the turn off, and there were flags and signs, but we couldn't tell what they meant and so stupidly ignored them. We got to the beach and it was deserted. I remember being dumbfounded – it was paradise, and empty. Everyone had vanished and we had it to ourselves. Stupid people. Our luck was in! I hoisted on my flippers, put on my goggles, and waded into the iridescent blue waters to swim, gleefully doing lengths parallel to the shoreline because there were no kids splashing around. It was midway through my second length of front crawl when I turned to face the ocean. But rather than seeing blue skies, I came face-to-face with an eyeball a matter of inches away. And not a human one. A shark. In that moment I am sure there's a sane, rescue-yourself way to behave – the type of top tips they give in marine-life documentaries – but I am ashamed to say I did everything you shouldn't. That is, I had a meltdown, flapping and rushing to the shore crying. I flung myself on the sand with moments to spare, screaming. Tom, irritatingly, thought it was quite funny. But I have been permanently scarred by the experience and have since vowed never to swim in the sea again. Swimming pools only, thank you.

Pretty soon, I'd meet Scott Tepper working at the store, another addition to my handful of loyal, incredible lifetime friends. Scott was a buyer for a vendor at the time. He had a cheeky irreverence, a warm face, with brown hair and brown eyes, and a great sense of humour. Apart from anything else he was genuinely nice – which belied the fact that he was also a shrewd merchant to his core. Scott's demeanour shocks people sometimes. He's such a kind, self-effacing guy, but will not suffer fools gladly when tested either. He loves to shop, knows what he wants – cashmere and fur feature heavily in his wardrobe – and will also happily shop on your behalf (much of my clothing collection was purchased at his behest).

Scott was trying to sell his brand's sunglasses and ready-to-wear to Henri Bendel when we met, which included an unfortunate collection of reversible raincoats. He soon joined Henri Bendel's staff, and later Bergdorf Goodman, where he oversaw footwear buying. We're now back together and he heads up collaborations at Liberty and lives in London as my next-door neighbour in Marylebone.

Even in the early days at Henri Bendel, Scott and I were

co-conspirators. We'd gather in my office, cooking up plans to take over the world of retail, bouncing around ideas, navigating the madness together. I still turn to Scott for advice. He can spot a killer opportunity at fifty paces, and often plays the bad cop to my good cop in difficult negotiating situations. He's got a unique combination of enthusiasm, open-mindedness and 'blue sky' thinking, where anything is possible – but often with incredibly shrewd instincts. He'll suggest a brand collaboration and you'll wonder, 'Why didn't I think of that?!'

Twenty years in as friends, and we boss each other around in the way that old married couples do. I tell him off for his cocktail consumption, he tells me off for being too nice. He loves a fitness fad, and is always on a strict regime; meanwhile, he laughs at my limited diet (I only like chicken, and bacon at a push. No spicy food, either). As friends and colleagues for the better part of twenty-five years, we've experienced the highs and lows together. We've travelled extensively. Scott has, and always will, love a drink and a party. And long may it continue . . .

***

One of The Limited Inc.'s early moves in 1990 was to leave the original store, built by Henri Bendel himself in 1913, and relocate to 712 Fifth Avenue near 56th Street. To their credit they'd selected a historic building in keeping with Bendel's former store spirit – a property set in two landmark New York City buildings, the former Rizzoli Building (712 Fifth Avenue) and former Coty Building (714 Fifth Avenue). The five-storey building featured beautiful Lalique windows, which were rediscovered during the restoration. It had four floors and a spectacular atrium with balconies, and (exciting to The Limited Inc.) 35,000 square feet of selling space. It was incredible.

The other new Henri Bendel locations weren't so successful. One of my earliest meetings was dedicated to discussing precisely what that Ohio flagship would look like. I immediately thought the idea was misguided. They also opened one flagship in a regional Boston mall, nowhere near the centre of the place that people actually shopped.

Everything about The Limited Inc. and the way they handled things was different. They took the iconic, but understated, Henri Bendel brown-and-white stripe motif, and exploded it everywhere in stores, applying it to drapes, to walls, to teapots – you name it.

They also rushed into their big plans. The years 1995 to 1998 saw the rapid expansion, and eventual contraction, of Henri Bendel. They hired Ted Marlow as president (and money man) for the store, and Angela Ahrendts to direct the purchase and launch of the new brand – bringing over teams from her former company Donna Karan, but then closing the label when it didn't work immediately. Many of the new locations were also closed soon after, eventually shrinking back to a single store, which is when Ted and Angela departed.

My first sphere of influence was the beauty hall, in which I set about creating a department that specialized in unique brands with limited distribution. I made this the USP of Henri Bendel, launching brands like MAC, Kevyn Aucoin, Laura Mercier, Trish McEvoy, Benefit and new fragrances by niche brands like Annick Goutal. I also introduced makeup artist's events, parties and trunk shows.

It was good timing to focus on these niche brands, because there were major shifts in the beauty market at that time. Consumers were bored of the sameness of faceless blockbuster brands. They wanted to relate to real people, and – answering this – a whole new wave of new makeup-artist and hair-technician-fronted brands started appearing. The person, or personality, became the core of these brands, which only added to their relatable appeal. This was the era of Bobbi Brown, Trish McEvoy, and Laura Mercier. They were so hot that many of the beauty conglomerates swooped in quickly to buy them.

The key to this new wave of brands was that their message was less about 'magic' and more about practical expert advice. In other words: 'This is what you got, honey. Let's help you be the best you can be.' It really resonated with people. It became a movement – people were tired of all the wild claims.

Carol Shaw, a working makeup artist in 1990, at the time founded LORAC cosmetics for sensitive skin, and was one of the leaders of this new wave. The first time she did an in-store appearance at Henri Bendel's beauty floor, I remember walking past as she exclaimed to a customer: 'Those are your eyebrows! Sorry! That's all I can do!' It was refreshing, and a world away from the product launches at Bloomingdale's, which had ridiculous names and made ridiculous claims.

I also met makeup artists Trish McEvoy and Bobbi Brown who'd set up lines at this time – though Bobbi's range of lipsticks had launched at Bergdorf Goodman, not in Henri Bendel. I've become friends with both Trish and Bobbi over the years and we've worked together numerous times on their respective brands. Both of them championed that same sense of reality, in beauty and education, which was really appealing to consumers. Today, Bobbi's makeup sales at Liberty of London (I got her line eventually!) top £1 million a year. Trish McEvoy is also a bestseller.

I still remember meeting Trish in the early days. Her husband was Doctor Sherman, famous for setting up the first 'medispa' in New York. Rumours were rife that Trish was developing a cosmetics line and trialling at her husband's clinic, which was the hottest joint in town since introducing the 'medical facial' concept. I invented a skin ailment to get an appointment and check out the products, which turned out to be amazing. The problem? Everyone wanted them. Pretty soon, I was begging Trish to sell her line to me. Trish, a dark-haired, petite, ultra-groomed and softly-spoken woman, kept on shying away. We'd meet repeatedly, for months. On each occasion she'd say, 'Ed, it's not the time.' In the end, I remember sitting across a table from her in a café. She was sitting down in front of me with two giant Chanel cuffs on, and thumped them down, giving me a steely look. I knew in that moment that the air had changed. 'Ed, now is *the time*,' she said. Paused. And we both burst out laughing.

She was right, as it turned out.

We launched the products in Henri Bendel. Typically back then, with new product launches we expected to do $5,000 in the first week. I got a call after the first day from a buyer. I was in Los Angeles on a buying trip and could barely believe my ears. 'Ed, we did $10,000 on our first day.' We could barely keep the product on the shop floor. Today, Trish is a longtime friend and business collaborator. We joke, each time we see each other, how well preserved we are. 'Ed, you look exactly the same!' Trish is also one of the few people I trust in the industry. I remember one of my earlier fitness trainers at this time had been suffering with AIDS – a potential death knell to his income. He seemed to be losing weight and suddenly started getting skin lesions. Pretty soon, he had one on his face and was desperately worried. How could he continue to work, and get his much-needed income, with this? This was a particular problem in a profession that was all about health. Trish was the only person I trusted. I took him to her to find products which could help mask the lesions, enabling him to work for a few more crucial months to fund his treatment. I'll never forget that act of kindness of hers.

Bobbi Brown would also develop into a lifelong friend. Bobbi, a working makeup artist at the time, had recently launched a line of lipsticks which she sold exclusively to Bergdorf Goodman, but eventually to me at Henri Bendel stores outside New York City. I loved her because she had a softness and realness to her, but was also very sharp. She was also 100 per cent about product, and not about ego. All she's ever done is focus on making great products since, which is perhaps why she's been so successful.

Many brands at this time also worked the whole behind-the-scenes expert theme, connecting it to real professionals working in studios and in the industry. Suddenly all this backstage glamour had become incredibly seductive to people. No one capitalized on this fervour more than MAC, which became nothing short of a global phenomenon shortly after its launch in Henri Bendel in 1989.

MAC's whole selling point was that it worked under studio lighting and under all conditions. Photographer Frank Toskan and salon owner Frank Angelo founded MAC (Makeup Art Cosmetics) in Toronto. From the get-go, when these Canadians came to New York, and to Henri Bendel in 1989, there was a buzz around this ultra-inclusive, cosmopolitan, fashion-inspired line of limitless shades (MAC's tag line, famously, is 'All ages. All races. All sexes'). It had already been attracting celebrity fans such as Madonna,

Above: Here I am as a baby, being startled by my big sister!

Right: My interest in swimming started at an early age.

Below: My mum and dad on North Shore, Long Island, in 1953.

Right: Me aged four or five in the back garden with my mum and sister. I clearly had a future in fashion.

Left: Mum and us kids at Southold beach, Long Island, 1963. Jamie's in the crib!

Right: Me drinking peaches in champagne at eleven!

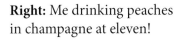

Left: With my beloved Aunt Hedi.

Right: In the 1970s, with big hair.

Left: At the Munich Olympics in 1972.

Right: My dear friend Danny in Florida. Good times!

Left: Everyone looked like this in the eighties . . . Unfortunately.

Below: Me and Tom, my partner of eighteen years, at a New Year's Eve party on the beach at Montauk.

Right: With Angela Ahrendts on a buying trip to Milan.

Below: All in black. A Henri Bendel buying trip to Berlin.

Bottom: With Danuta Ryder, Visual and Image Director at Henri Bendel.

Above: With Donald Trump and his wife Melania at a Henri Bendel party.

Right: Iman at her birthday party in a subterranean restaurant in the East Village, New York.

Below: With Quentin Crisp on his ninetieth birthday at my 11th Street apartment.

Above: In the Henri Bendel store with Monica Lewinsky discussing her handbag line.

Right: With Diane von Furstenberg at the opening event for her shop-in-shop at Henri Bendel.

Right: Me, having been named as a 'Gay of the Year' by *Out* magazine.

Below: With Manolo Blahnik and his niece, Kristina Blahnik (far left), at the opening of World of Manolo Blahnik at Liberty.

Princess Diana, and a host of others. Henri Bendel promptly became MAC's first US stockist. Though Frank and Frank, as they were known, were miles apart from their wild image. They were remarkably quiet, introverted and even guarded. I imagine they channelled all their extroversion into the brand. I'd go to Canada to spend time with them, and reassure them we had their best interests at heart. I knew I'd won them over when I found myself going to gay Toronto strip-joints with them after a few drinks.

Part of what people loved about MAC was its playfulness, which is why, in 1995, when we came to announce the company's new spokesperson at Henri Bendel with a six-foot-four-inch-tall drag queen named RuPaul, we went all out. It was outrageous! RuPaul showed up in a giant wig, towering over everybody, and the crowd went wild. The response to that line was like a high-speed train. It just exploded.

We ran with its exuberant spirit. Later, we'd have MAC windows on Fifth Avenue featuring live-action body-painting on models. There would be crowds outside glued to the glass. Other times we'd have go-go boys dancing on the streets, dressed as cupids in nothing but G-strings. In the windows, meanwhile, they'd be bathing naked in tubs with rubber ducks. The irreverence and fun of that brand provided constant creative fodder for truly cool parties.

The beauty of working in retail is that the proof is in the pudding – and if something is working, your bosses will generally let you continue and go as far as you want. There are no politics. If it works, they don't question it. The gist is 'Keep doin' what you're doin'!' until it breaks. At least, that's how it worked with my bosses at the time, Ted Marlow and Angela Ahrendts. They gave free rein of the store.

As the store, at large, continued to go through an awkward transition under The Limited Inc., and sales were rocky in other departments, I was behind the most profitable floors. As a result of beauty's success, they loaded me up with new departments to run.

Buying ready-to-wear fashion was a transition for me. I'm not a natural fashionista and while I've learned to have an eye, and evolve a basic personal uniform, the art of ready-to-wear retail was a different ball game. Selling fashion is different to selling beauty. It's a much more emotive and intimate product, and subject to many more variables. You market it differently, too.

There are also way more egos to deal with! With beauty people, what you see is what you get. Less so with fashion – but luckily I've always been very good at masquerading. I'd turn up to my first fashion shows in New York Fashion Week, take my front-row seat and be furiously scribbling notes – little did anyone know that I was writing grocery lists ('Buy cigarettes. Pick up milk'). I've always seen fashion shows as mostly entertainment only, and still do. The business and the buy is what matters.

Fashion shows were another social terrain I had to learn to navigate though, fast. When I think of things I first started wearing to shows it makes me laugh. I'd go in sweat pants. But by the time I went to the Paris fashion shows, I knew enough was enough. I went to Jeffrey's in the Meatpacking District and bought a suit, and continued to smarten up my act.

I did learn to buy fashion, too. It's not rocket science. You evolve not only a taste level, but learn to buy enough of the things that people will actually buy, with a sprinkling of pieces that will get you attention and put you in magazines. And I learned to identify what would appeal to our customer.

I also learned to love the fashion press. They spotted me for the imposter I initially was, but I eventually won them over. I like to think I did, anyway. I remember being devastated by one of the earlier pieces in the style section of *The New York Times* about all my activities as new general manager at Henri Bendel. It was quite snooty, not only about a new designer collaboration I'd launched, but also about the whole direction I was taking the store in. 'In its heyday Henri Bendel never needed to rely on buzz', it said. 'Buzz', written with disdain, was framed as a terribly gauche thing – ignoring that the store was finally doing better in sales at that time thanks to these new additions.

I nearly cried when I read that article. I've since established great relationships with other fashion journalists. Sometimes unlikely circumstances have prompted introductions. Ex-*New York Times* fashion critic Cathy Horyn and I were trapped at an airport in a snowstorm en route to London from New York one ill-fated fashion week, and after that we spoke often for stories. I met *New York Times* journalist Ruth La Ferla outside the New York Fashion Week tents, while huddling over a cigarette in the rain. We shared a cab to the next show and today are great friends.

Regardless of whether they are writing about me and my store or not, I have come to believe in the importance of being not only genial, but also open (this is actually my policy across the board). Be it fashion person, beauty person, journalist, vendor or assistant, I've found that being kind always trumps being difficult. And being open, too – whether it's meetings, phone calls or lunches. All these things can lead to brilliant opportunities and relationships. Besides, I could never pull off frosty.

For all the allure of fashion buying, I still believe that the best training in retail is actually to be a cosmetic buyer. The fact is that you're always selling the same product, the same red lipstick, and the same goop. Every six months you have to figure out a way to sell the same product, which means you have to be creative, and you always have to invent a sense of novelty.

I also like that nothing is ever about the designer's ego in beauty – it's about what sells and what doesn't. You can't go to Alexander Wang and say: 'Alexander, give me some new colour clothes'. He gives you the seasonal colour palette, there it is.

What it comes down to in beauty is a real-estate game. Everything is centred on profitability per square foot and how you market it. That's why beauty brands are so obsessed with their position on the shop floor. Ninety per cent of the time, beauty shopping is not destination. It's an impulse. Which is why the beauty department is always on the ground floor, by the front door. It's to capture all that impulse. That's why those people are annoying you all the time (people like me at Macy's!) with spritzers.

As a result, many brands vie for real estate on beauty floors. It's an aggressively fought-over territory. Major cosmetics houses will often occupy prime territory. Some of their concessions are like glowing spaceships – large, theatrical and enticing. When they're in stores that aren't concession-based, they also cleverly insist that buyers buy entire product ranges rather than cherry-pick and edit, as has become popular with the newer wave of 'curated' beauty retailers.

At Liberty, it's worth noting, we restrict the size of every counter. Each brand – whether Kiehl's, NARS, Frederic Malle or Diptyque – gets the same square footage so that no brand overwhelms the other. It's the 'Street of Shops' all over – in other words, we try to create a sense of multiple small boutiques. It's what our customer comes to us for – variety, and a sharp edit, apart from anything else.

***

Working with Angela Ahrendts and Ted Marlow was an experience. Not to mention a lesson in retail from two of the greatest out there, even if it was all too brief.

Angela is a force, as simple as that, with an incredible energy and focus that I've not seen before, or since. When she joined Henri Bendel she was as polished, poised and glamorous as she is now. Even then she was a big name to watch in the industry – I think she always knew she was destined for more than the cornfields of the American Midwest, where she grew up.

Angela and I often travelled to Europe together, to buy collections and take private label meetings for the Henri Bendel brand. Working with her was always incredibly fast-paced. Think seven cities in seven days. I remember being on an overnight flight to Milan one time. I figured that was long enough to get a good sleep, so I ordered a glass of wine and took a sleeping pill (the red-eye sedative of champions). But she got back from the bathroom and turned to me, reaching for papers in her briefcase. 'Right, so now a nice stretch of work before a quick two-hour sleep, yes?' I was already feeling drowsy from the sleeping pill, but managed to prop my eyes open somehow.

When we landed she would continue at that rate. She'd get up at 5 a.m. to jog. When we went to appointments there was none of the Italian or French preamble. She'd be able to spot the two singularly good items on a rack in seconds, then move on to the next.

I remember the morning of one of the Henri Bendel clothing brand launches in New York; Ted and I saw her running around looking uncharacteristically dishevelled. 'Angela!' Ted said. 'You look like you've been up all night!' She whipped around, quick as a flash, and quipped, 'Third in a row,' with a wink.

Angela may have been demanding to work for, but she also had a terrifically sharp sense of humour and immense humility. It was Angela, years later, who'd encourage me to take over Liberty of London – cautioning me on the culture shock of working with a historic brand, as well as the perils of London's sky-high rents, while extolling the UK's virtues. She was also the one who promoted me regularly during my time at Henri Bendel, when she could have had her pick of many more experienced candidates. And for that, I could not be more thankful.

This confidence peaked when she handed me buying responsibility for all of the departments. Little did she know, at the time my eighteen-year relationship with Tom was coming to an end. I was keeping it as slick and together at work as ever, but at home I was a total mess. When you're ending any kind of relationship of that length, stress levels are off the chart.

I remember it all came to a head after I had been drinking excessively for weeks and checked into St Vincent's Hospital New York with a 41-degree (105 degrees Fahrenheit) temperature. I stayed in for eleven days with alcohol poisoning and passed it off as stomach flu to the management team (silver lining, I lost ten pounds – the best diet ever). During that rehabilitative stay at St Vincent's – unaware of what had really happened – Angela called to promote me to buying director of Henri Bendel.

In retrospect, that was exactly what I needed, and a huge vote of confidence. That strange surreal moment where I got a massive career boost pulled me out of a black hole and propelled me forward. I laughed, a little too hysterically, when I got off the phone on the ward. Life is strange. Despite the aftermath of emotional fallout from my break-up with Tom, we too became friends again and now speak almost every day. Tom takes care of my affairs in New York, is my memory at the end of a phone when I cannot recall restaurant names – we don't even say 'Hello', but fire straight into whatever question we have in mind. And we still share a glass of wine, or five, when I'm back in New York. We're best friends, in other words. The first wives never go away . . .

Angela's time at Henri Bendel was short-lived. By 1998 the private label brand wasn't growing as fast as The Limited Inc. liked and the board members made a decision to shut it down. But it all worked out for Angela in the end. Last I read, her golden hello for her recent move to Apple alone was $68 million in shares. (Though, to be fair, I'd say that's an accurate estimation of her value. She's worth every cent.)

In the interim – in other words, before creating the Burberry Empire – Angela left Henri Bendel and was promptly snatched up in 1998 by Fifth & Pacific Companies, where she ended up as executive vice president of Liz Claiborne. Ted Marlow and I continued to run Henri Bendel for a while, before Ted handed the store to me – he left to be senior vice president of Saks Fifth Avenue in the same year.

Ted Marlow has only risen since he left Henri Bendel, which again, to me, is not surprising. After Saks Fifth Avenue, he became vice president of merchandising, product development and marketing at the women's clothing chain Chico's. More recently, he's served as executive director of business development at Urban Outfitters Inc., and now is CEO of Urban Outfitters Group.

Looking at him, you wouldn't guess he worked in fashion retail. He has quite a mountain-man appearance – he's six feet three inches tall, and during his time at Henri Bendel sported a full beard and wore plaid shirts. He didn't even live in New York City. Instead, he lived in the countryside in a rustic house with moose heads mounted on the walls. He's always been very calm and rational, but behind this he is an extremely tenacious retailer with very incisive taste. At Henri Bendel he was key to my success because he wasn't a micromanager. If something worked, his only message was: 'Great, explode it.' He trusted you to use your instincts.

We still share a laugh about the retail business. He recently drove past Liberty of London and saw sale signs in the window. He didn't come in and see me, but instead emailed me: 'I just drove past Liberty and saw your discount signs. Your stuff is obviously as precious as mine.' I spat out my coffee laughing! As retailers, you have to have a healthy sense of humour about such things.

Ted left Henri Bendel in 1998 after the store closures. He delivered news of my appointment to general manager in a meeting one chilly November afternoon in his office before a statement was due to be put out to press. He sat across a desk, and all of a sudden the honks and street noise of New York City outside evaporated into a wooly blur. 'I'm handing it over to you,' he said. I left the store in a total daze. What had just happened? I was meeting Scott for dinner that evening and told him, still not taking it in myself. He nearly choked on his wine: '*Ed!* You've got a whole store! *A whole store!*'

I felt like a child who'd been left the keys to a mansion, and a credit card, while my parents went away. What was I going to do with it?

***

From the moment I took the reins at Henri Bendel in 1998, I knew I had a challenge on my hands. All the changes, the growing, the shrinking, and the revolving door of management had significantly diminished the store's power.

In the meantime, our competitors had become powerhouses; all had vast marketing and store budgets. They were all on our doorstep and we were – comparatively – tiny. A small minnow swimming among great whites.

Of all the retail battlegrounds in history, few have been fiercer than New York City during the late 1990s. Riding high on a decade of economic prosperity, luxury fashion and beauty brands had exploded all over the place, launching flagships across the globe, peddling logoed handbags, totes and headbands to a baying mob. Tom Ford had been named creative director of Gucci and was overseeing its glamorous renaissance and expansion. Louis Vuitton was recalibrating itself, scaling back distribution to create a standalone army of logo-bedecked Louis Vuitton temples. Then there was Prada, the hottest luxury brand of the moment, whose black nylon rucksacks were practically a uniform at this time. The economy was booming and every New York department store wanted a piece of the pie.

Each one vied for a specific niche of consumer. Bloomingdale's was pizzazz, blockbuster and youth. Saks Fifth Avenue had the mid-level luxury market covered, and the out-of-towners. Bergdorf Goodman had New York society wrapped up. Barneys was all quirk and fashion lovers.

How do you compete in these circumstances? You get creative, that's what. We set about creating our own news by playing to our strengths – that is, rejecting the 'mega-brand' and concession model altogether, and instead focusing on finding new, hot, niche, and never-before-seen labels, international brands and designers, and exploding them in New York. We threw in the most outrageous windows and glittering parties we could along the way and, most importantly, a sense of retail theatre.

Somehow that feeling of being the underdog helped us be more creative and take more risks. We had nothing to lose, after all. We were irreverent and fun, and this seemed to chime with the mood of New Yorkers who came and partied with us.

By the dawn of the 2000s, Henri Bendel was riding high with the best of them; a hub for whacky parties, celebrities, new collections and windows. And the tills were ringing. Not bad for a store a fraction of its neighbours' size!

This was the era of *Sex and the City* in New York, which helped. HBO's *Sex and the City* was a cultural phenomenon from the second it hit TV screens in 1998. In New York, it kickstarted a virtual revolution in fashion and luxury. Women not only became more experimental and confident with the way they dressed; shopping, and especially shopping for luxury fashion, became a cult pursuit.

Sex and the City drove the It-shoe and It-bag phenomena, the insatiable lust for statement, must-have pieces, no matter what the price (unsurprisingly, this marked the beginning of massive price hikes in designer accessories, which have only continued to rise). Manolo Blahnik, Jimmy Choo and Christian Louboutin became global brands as a result.

Henri Bendel became the *Sex and the City* store, in all its pink tutu glory. We hosted parties and trunk shows, and became known for selling the newest hot fashion designers again. Patricia Field, the stylist and costume designer for the show, was a regular at our events – not only as a guest, but also launching her own accessories line in-store in 2002 (attended by the cast: Sarah Jessica Parker, Kim Cattrall, Cynthia Nixon and Kristin Davis). Pat is lovable for her utter fearlessness. She's never done anything by the book, and what's more, she's a survivor. She's still here! And still sporting that amazing pillarbox-red hair.

This was also the time when vintage fashion was on the rise, not only prompting people to hunt for original vintage pieces, but also creating renewed interest in previously iconic retro labels.

Diane von Furstenberg was one of the beneficiaries of this. By 1997, fashionable society girls had started hunting out her original wrap dresses. Meanwhile, Tom Ford, designing at Gucci, had re-established a love for all things seventies and Studio 54. Diane was a poster girl for this era, and felt inspired to relaunch her line. I heard about this and right away sought her out. I remember stepping into her New York townhouse in the West Village, with a reflecting pool in the entrance and her giant portrait by Andy Warhol on the wall. Diane has an amazing manner about her, which is at once very down-to-earth and yet hugely glamorous. There she was, tossing her hair back and forth, and then suddenly she said, 'Let's talk business.' I was thinking, 'Alright!'

We hit it off immediately, and I ended up staying the whole afternoon. She'd been so smart about the whole new collection, making sure all the iconic pieces were there. We held several parties for Diane, including her initial launch, which was attended by Calvin Klein and Bianca Jagger: our very own Studio 54 reunion! It marked the beginning of what was a long Henri Bendel relationship.

Stephen Burrows was another revival triumph. Geraldine Stutz at Henri Bendel had been one of the first to champion Stephen's disco gowns in the seventies, by giving him his own shop in-store. Stephen was one of the legendary Versailles Five, the troop of American designers who, in 1973, were pitched against five of Paris's finest designers – Yves Saint Laurent, Christian Dior, Hubert de Givenchy, Pierre Cardin and Emanuel Ungaro – in a stand-off Palace of Versailles fashion show conceived by American fashion publicist Eleanor Lambert and the event's curator, Gerald Van der Kemp.

The event was created to raise funds for Versailles' palace restoration in France and saw American designers Bill Blass, Halston, Stephen Burrows, Anne Klein and Oscar de la Renta compete against the French with fashion – the Americans famously won with modern, fresh, clean designs. They all received a ton of adulation and exposure as a result.

Stephen had practically disappeared from the fashion scene by 2002, but references to his work and aesthetic had started appearing in collections everywhere. Scott and I kept seeing his signatures on the catwalks, and over drinks one night it hit Scott: 'Wait a second,' he said. 'Where *is* Stephen?'

We tracked him down at his home and went to talk to him in person about relaunching his label in our Henri Bendel atelier. While taken aback at first, he agreed. Collections had been produced in Henri Bendel's atelier before, and we loved the idea of going back to this tradition – though it wasn't without its challenges. Stephen is famous for his silk jersey, expertly cut pieces in rainbow hues that have a signature 'lettuce' scalloped hem, which gives them a terrific sense of movement. Finding fabric wasn't hard, but finding special scissors to create the hem twenty years later was. I remember sending assistants all over Manhattan on a hunt to find just the right scissors – those damned scissors – but we got there! And the new collection was stunning. Stephen was successful with the Henri Bendel line for some years after that.

We launched the collection with a party, naturally. This was hosted by André Leon Talley, editor-at-large at *Vogue*, who wore a large, dramatic cape and swooped around the room in his beloved, inimitably grandiose style. It was one of the biggest parties of this time at Henri Bendel and showed the huge amount of support Stephen had from the fashion community, and fans, for his designs. Anna Sui, Iman, Lou Reed, Diane von Furstenberg, Rick Owens, Daryl Kerrigan, Pat Cleveland, Carolina Herrera and Hamish Bowles were there.

I remember Iman's arrival. The doors parted for the elevator and she appeared in this incredible canary-yellow, bias-cut evening gown; everyone gasped. She was utterly breathtaking. Everyone came to Stephen's party – not just celebrities and fashion designers, but noted fashion press from Suzy Menkes to Cathy Horyn, which to me was also a turning point for the store. We were being taken seriously in fashion again. After twenty years of Stephen's obscurity, *New York* magazine described it as 'one of the biggest comebacks in fashion history'. Meanwhile, *Vogue* called our event the 'party of the season'.

I continued this thread in the early 2000s, trying to bring Henri Bendel more of the high fashion credibility it had enjoyed under Geraldine Stutz. I got us involved in the Hyères fashion festival, the prestigious annual awards held in a small coastal town in the South of France for up-and-coming talent in the fashion industry, widely known as a platform for the future big names of the fashion world. We became an official partner, launching the Henri Bendel award.

One of our key tactics for making Henri Bendel relevant again was to seek out hot new labels before anyone else had discovered them, and bring them to New York. I would go on frequent escapades to Tokyo, Los Angeles, Australia – you name it – in search of cool stuff.

We were the first to stock labels like Marni, Ann Demeulemeester, and Roberto Cavalli in the US. We were the first to go to Sydney and Melbourne and find all the great labels there. We went everywhere people didn't go, essentially.

Another way we found new stuff was with the Henri Bendel Open Call: an open audition for new designers where anyone could bring their product to see us and get feedback. We still do this at Liberty of London. Open Call was originally introduced by Geraldine Stutz, and was fundamental to getting new talent into stores.

Some of our runaway successes came from the most unexpected places. I remember when an agent of ours first started talking about what was then a little casual line in Los Angeles called Juicy (later Juicy Couture), founded by friends Pamela Skaist-Levy and Gela Nash-Taylor in the mid-nineties. She had been seeing people walking all around Santa Monica wearing their signature candy-coloured T-shirts and later the now-signature velour and terry-cloth Juicy Couture tracksuits. They were fun, and very tongue-in-cheek, with funny slogans on them such as 'Dump Him', 'I Want Candy' and 'Smells Like Couture'. Local celebrities had started wearing pieces. In local boutiques, meanwhile, one table quickly became a corner, and whole sections of stores were dedicated to the label. We swooped in there quickly, bringing their line to New York, and people went nuts for it. There was something about it that sat so perfectly with the changes in fashion then. Los Angeles was seen as very glamorous, and celebrity dressing was having more of an impact on trends thanks to the celebrity lifestyle weeklies. There was also a general casualization of fashion happening at that time, and the relaxed, but sexy, Los Angeles look really resonated. Juicy Couture got picked up in every fashion magazine, especially after celebrities were spotted wearing pieces. Pretty soon, those cheeky tracksuits were a uniform, not just among Los Angeles celebrities like Madonna, J. Lo and the Hiltons, but were a worldwide must-have. For better, or worse . . .

Another Los Angeles designer we had championed early on at Henri Bendel was Rick Owens. I remember first going to see him in Los Angeles in 1995. This was before Los Angeles was rehabbed; downtown Hollywood was practically a warzone. Rick lived with his enigmatic French wife Michèle Lamy, who presided over Les Deux Cafés, which was the coolest club-meets-salon-meets-cabaret in town, a nightly hangout for Madonna, Lenny Kravitz, Courtney Love, Sofia Coppola, and Tim Burton among others.

Michèle and Rick lived across the street, where they had converted a series of dishevelled storefronts into a home and studio. I remember walking into Rick's studio to see hangers strung from the ceiling holding his black draped jersey and fishtails – they looked like black bats suspended from the roof of a cave, very fitting for Rick's gothic personality. As it turned out, Rick was developing his signature bias-cut jersey pieces and fishtails, carefully experimenting with how the weight of the fabric hung by doing just that – hanging them from the ceiling. I bought the collection soon after.

Rick and I have stayed friends over the years. He's one of those great straightforward, no-nonsense fashion people where there are no games, which is so rare. I see him at shows in Paris and he always has his signature black mane of hair, though he seems to swing between being an incredibly pumped-up, muscle-bound Rick, or a gracefully wiry 'Rock God' Rick.

We stock Rick Owen's pieces in Liberty of London and they continue to be bestsellers, not only to our young customers but also to older women. There's an art to cutting T-shirt fabric to drape in the way that it does in his clothes, which people rarely appreciate until they try it on. They're incredibly sexy.

One of my riskiest moves at Henri Bendel was to stock Monica Lewinsky's bag line, but this again put us in the headlines. In 1999 and 2000, Monica had been laying low in Los Angeles since the Clinton-gate scandal, but started making handbags to occupy her time. The label was intentionally very far from anything you'd imagine of the tabloid 'Monica Lewinsky' cartoon. They were hobo-ish patchwork and crochet sewing bags, which simply had a label 'Made with Love by Monica'. Our Los Angeles agent showed them to me and I liked them. And, more importantly, I liked Monica. I asked her in to meet me in New York in our offices, and she had the most incredibly wry sense of humour. Plus, she was smart. It still makes me laugh that reports often refer to her as stupid. She has a BA Honours degree, a Masters in psychology from the London School of Economics, and her first internship was at the White House. How much smarter could she be?

It's sad to me, too, that in our culture, nothing like that is forgotten if you're a woman. Even now, Monica is stuck in time, and it's over a decade ago. It's the same thing in England with Christine Keeler, famed for her involvement in the Profumo affair. You still get those mean-spirited articles in showbiz updates online, papping her another year older in the supermarket and comparing it with the iconic nude chair photo taken in 1963 – Lord knows I'd hate to have pictures of me with grey hair compared with my moustached, muscle-bound eighties youth. Monica is forever trapped in 1998.

So how great was it to see an article written by Monica in *Vanity Fair* this year? She has had enough of being silent, and has finally decided to put the past to rest.

An even greater joy is that Monica and I have been reconnected. She loves London and spends quite a lot of time here – and it's great to report that she is as witty, quick, funny and warm as I remember.

When we met she was more petite than I imagined, but still curvy, with her classic black hair, a crisp white shirt and black skirt. She cut right to the elephant in the room: 'Well, you know, after everything I've been through . . .' she joked when I asked her what made her move from politics to patchwork. We agreed to put the bags on sale as a trial, with no labelling, to see if there was a real appetite. It was an experiment, and lo and behold, they sold really well. After a while, we were selling so many that I suggested to her that we do an in-store appearance, showing her new line as a proven commercial success. We used it as a platform to show the public a new iteration of brand 'Monica Lewinsky'.

Monica was understandably hesitant at appearing in public, but eventually she agreed. She showed up on the day with her mother, hyperventilating with fear, not least because of the crowds. We knew her appearance would get attention, but hadn't anticipated the avalanche that occurred that day. People started lining up at 3 a.m. the night before. We held the event on the fourth floor of the store and on the day the line went right down the stairs and out the front door, round the block and beyond. It was an absolute circus. There were camera crews, press – everybody. Of course there were tabloid reporters asking offensive questions, but overall the response was incredibly positive. Reporters kept on asking me why we'd worked with her and I replied again and again: 'It's because the bags sold!' They didn't seem to want to hear it.

It's nice to see people succeed in adversity and I'm always proud that we took that gamble with Monica.

After our collaboration, Monica and I stayed in touch. I was a friendly face she said 'hi' to in the West Village where we both lived. She even tried to set me up when I was single with some of her friends. I remember being in Gristedes buying groceries one day and her shouting at me across three cashier counters as we were in line. 'Hey Ed! Are you single right now? I'm having a party with some people on Friday and I want to introduce you!' It was a surreal moment. I didn't go but was touched (we all know the New York dating scene can be perilous).

In the early 2000s, the balance of power between the catwalks of Paris, Milan, New York and London was different to what it is now. Today, London is on par with the other fashion capitals and visited by all the top buyers and press every season. Meanwhile, London designers are sold globally along with the best of them.

But London's fashion scene was a few steps behind back then. The creativity and famous London edge was there, of course. Fashion buyers and editors went there to scope out new directional talent but few actually bought anything, purely because lots of these labels had not honed their production and deliveries, and many of the pieces – while daring and new – were not commercial enough to sell. I saw an opportunity for Henri Bendel here.

I made it my mission to introduce designers like Luella, Roland Mouret, Alice Temperley and Jonathan Saunders into the US.

I remember my first meeting with Roland Mouret, who from the get-go was as utterly charming as he is now, and produced female-friendly designs I knew would be a hit with our customers. Roland's skill is that he is flirtatious without being heavy-handed. He makes women feel great, and knows his customer. Even now at Liberty of London, we host Roland Mouret shopping evenings with him for VIP clients, throwing in glasses of champagne for a party feel.

To watch Roland with his customers is to see an expert at work. He is reassuring, complimentary, and they usually walk away with at least one purchase. In 2013, when he launched a capsule line with a cocktail at Liberty, we sold out in one night.

It's incredibly seductive as a selling tool having the creator of a product, of a makeup or clothing line, in-store to meet customers. It's one I use regularly now. If a designer or founder of a line is personable, it's a huge plus-point when I am considering buying them. I've never got the aloof, distanced designers. This is a business about clientele and embracing your customers and an education for the designer, meeting 'real' people who wear their clothes!

In many ways, Roland reminds me of an early Michael Kors. He, too, has always understood the art of selling, and befriending his clients. Kors is the ultimate in personal selling. Get him on any shop floor with his product and he'll be in the dressing room with his ladies singing Barbara Streisand, finding them just the right accessory. It's an absolute art. Not all the London designers were as finessed as Roland, though.

London Fashion Week was relatively chaotic – but full of energy. Shows didn't run on time as they (usually) do now, and were packed. Champagne circulating from about 10 a.m. daily helped to create a party atmosphere.

Then there was pricing. A lot of British designers, due to their small production runs, priced their collections very high. I remember talking to designer Alice Temperley about her beautifully embellished boho evening gowns, asking: 'Do we really need a three-tier beaded sleeve here? Could you do with two? I think that would have the same effect.'

Often this quirkiness was quite charming. I remember meeting a fresh-faced Katie Hillier and Luella Bartley. They'd brought their collection stuffed into a suitcase to meet me, and would bring out sweaters, explaining that the pony would eventually 'be on the top-right-hand side, by the chest' – leaving me to imagine what the tops I'd be buying would eventually look like. They learned quickly though, and most recently were appointed creative and design directors at Marc by Marc Jacobs. And besides, that collection was a hit.

I quickly realized that theatre was one other way we could recapture the spotlight for Henri Bendel. I'd learned first-hand from Bloomingdale's the art of theatrics and drama for selling a fragrance. While Bloomingdale's had got theirs down to a formula, I wanted to take this further and be a bit more creative. We started making the store windows a venue for live-action events and spectacles. Painted models, costumes, campness – you name it, we bought it in.

We hosted a Hugh Hefner personal appearance for the launch

of Playboy's fiftieth anniversary commemorative book with Hugh surrounded by Playboy bunnies. We created tons of specially commissioned memorabilia and knick-knacks, and crowds lined the block. Poor Hugh, the blonde models in their skyscraper heels towered over him – not that he was complaining.

We also worked the party scene, bringing the store back to life with flashbulbs and fizz. And boy, did we have some parties. There were parties for Roca Wear with Damon Dash. Heidi Klum showed up for her trainer David Kirsch's spa collection. Iman was a regular fixture during this time – one minute circulating at a party with champagne, the next camping out on the ground floor suggesting customers buy her book or makeup line: 'Dahling, this shade would suit you.'

It was at some of these parties that I experienced real moments of reflection. The shop floor would be so packed and I'd suddenly think: it's working! I'm onto something here and I want to run with it. Sales were improving. The store had a real buzz. We were moving in the right direction. Success like this, especially when it's hard won, is incredibly exhilarating. Some of these parties took my breath away.

Our crazy party for the launch of *Charlie's Angels* the movie, starring Lucy Liu, Drew Barrymore and Cameron Diaz, marked one of these moments. We did a collection and held a screening and party in-store. We thought the girls would do a drive-by (in other words, come in, have a picture taken, and stay for two minutes), but they were hardcore. They stayed up drinking and dancing on couches all night long. We ended up having to get security to stop more celebrities coming in! I remember Destiny's Child (before they were Destiny's Child) at the door. Thankfully we let them in –

before long they were big stars.

We continued this theme with much-imitated, regular-customer parties, called 'Girls Night Out'. These featured talks with Diane von Furstenberg about her comeback, or Iman on her amazing 'discovery' story, furnished with cheese cubes and wine, a potent cocktail for shopping splurges. They were intimate and fun, and women loved it. And, while they were having fun, they shopped.

It was all coming together. Even my love life was getting a boost, courtesy of *Out* magazine. I was featured in 2001's 'Out 100', the magazine's round up of the most influential gay success stories. The photo was black and white and really quite flattering (I still use it now). My listing garnered a lot of romantic interest, as well as putting Bendel's further in the spotlight.

This is when my job changed in my mind. It shifted from being about product, to being about marketing. Everything I was doing was about brand building, rather than strictly retail.

We didn't make a lot of money out of these silly launches – how many people are going to buy a piece of *Charlie's Angels* clothing? Really? But they got our name out there. I learned a lot about how much of the right kind of attention the right kind of event brings to the store. I've never forgotten that. With any venture, besides questioning if something will sell now, I ask what the story is. Is there a story? How do we use this to raise our profile? I've developed a strange algorithm: product + publicity + commerciality = winner.

Of course, not all my time at the helm at Henri Bendel was glitz and glamour. Slap bang in the middle of my tenure in 2001, September 11 made a large, sombre dent in the frivolities. The disaster swept away lower Manhattan's, not to mention national, morale for a long while – it made New Yorkers, a typically fierce bunch, lose their bravado temporarily too, before rallying.

Beyond the clouds of dusty fog, the economy of New York and retail suffered hugely. I remember on the day, I'd been meeting Trip Gabriel from *The New York Times* and designer Tiffany Dubin, when my assistant came in and told us: 'We've been attacked.' I then, in a state of shock, had to find a way to evacuate five hundred staff and get them home safely. It was complete bedlam. People were experiencing every emotion under the sun, from hysteria, to tears, to silence.

The hardest thing for me was that my brother worked in one of the towers. By miraculous coincidence he'd been in a meeting uptown that day, but I spent hours panicking, not knowing if he was dead. But I needed to stay outwardly strong for my staff.

It was like that for everyone. Those Twin Towers were so important in the New York ecosystem – three thousand people worked there; everyone had a connection to someone who worked there. Everyone was worrying about someone.

The streets were surreal. People walked around stunned, like zombies. The dividing line beyond which people were allowed to walk freely was 14th Street; I lived below that, so was able to walk past the barriers to my apartment. My apartment, too, had its own eerie feel. I was on the top floor, my windows looking south to where the Twin Towers used to be, and in the aftermath there were only towers of smoke. The neighbourhood was also creepy – no cars, no traffic, meant that the usual New York street orchestra of horns, brakes and shouting, was temporarily quietened. All you could hear were ambulances and helicopters.

The days immediately following the attack were a blur. Lower Manhattan, including where I lived in the Village, was shrouded in a dust-fog. There was dust everywhere. Meanwhile, people vanished from the stores. Mayor Bloomberg, to his credit, supported businesses in New York by encouraging New Yorkers to shop. It inspired quite a sense of patriotism in businesses too. We stuck up American flags in our windows. It also engendered an incredible sense of pride and kindness in New Yorkers. Everyone wanted to help. Neighbourhoods became your focus – how you could help the firefighters and emergency services. Tom and I volunteered near St Vincent's Hospital and the scenes were like nothing else I'd ever seen. There wasn't enough space for all the casualties, so patients were laid out on beds in the street, with blood all over them, exposed injuries, and in extreme pain. It's so strange, even now, to think that actually happened. The effect on the US psyche was profound. Prior to 9/11, New Yorkers in particular prided themselves on their invincibility. We had one of the most powerful metropolises in the most powerful nation of the world so the attack was received with stunned disbelief. Many in the wake of the events became wary of living in such a high profile – and therefore prime target – city. I remember some of my employees moving back to their parents in the Midwest. New York for the most part, thankfully, has since bounced back and is still as proud, loud and vibrant as ever.

All parties must come to an end, and that's essentially what happened. By 2004, I'd turned Henri Bendel around. 'Dog whistle fashion' it wasn't – but it was relevant. It was at this point that The Limited Inc. took a renewed interest in growth and expansion. As owners of Victoria's Secret they knew the underwear brand business inside out, and their next strategy was to build out Henri Bendel as an underwear and homewares brand. They were returning to their chain idea, in other words, but in a different iteration.

When The Limited Inc. told me about these plans, I realized that the bra business simply wasn't for me, so I jumped ship into the world of freelance – thankfully Angela Ahrendts was there to scoop me up.

CHAPTER 5

THE BERGDORF ERA: SWIMMING WITH THE BIG BOYS

'I knew it was time to take a breather when *Sex and the City* went off the air,' I joked in an interview with *Women's Wear Daily* when they announced my stepping down at Henri Bendel, using humour to brush off the overwhelming sadness.

I'd gone in at the bottom at Henri Bendel; I had worked my way up from beauty buyer to general manager. I'd poured my heart into the store, living its parties, staying up late, devoting sleepless nights to its success. I loved it. That's what happens with single-store businesses: they get into your soul and you become emotionally intertwined with their fate – or at least, that's always how it's been with me. I've since recognized the same thing at Liberty of London – the old Spook House has worked her magic well.

I left Henri Bendel, stepping outside the city gates, and suddenly all that love, and work, didn't seem to mean very much. My rational mind got it, of course. If you're a huge corporation you're never going to understand the rationale for a single-store business. Their main competency was lingerie, so it made sense to focus on leveraging that and expanding into chains.

Added to my slightly bruised ego was also a mild sense of panic. Non-compete clauses are such in retail that you can't just jump straight into another retail job. There I was, with a summer to kill, and very limited options.

At first, I embraced my newfound freedom. Brunch on Tuesdays, yay! Lie-ins, yay! Galleries in the afternoon, yay! And then the boredom set in. The truth is, I'm not great at having time off, and I was desperate for a project to occupy me.

I started interviewing at every store in the meantime, but nothing really appealed to me. I remember one ill-fated meeting with the CEO of another ailing Grande Dame department store in search of a revamp. Sat in a sweaty office among dusty desk ornaments, he turned to me and said: 'We're trying to make the store cool again. We even had Beyontz in the other week.' 'Beyontz?' I repeated back, puzzled, before it became clear he was referring to the global, international pop sensation Beyoncé. Poor guy. Needless to say, I took that as a bad omen. Plus, I wasn't ready to turn another ship around.

I was then approached by another major department store, which had been struggling with the fact that the two ends of their business, the buying division and the store division, did not communicate properly. More than that, both hated each other. They were creating a new bridging job – a role for an intermediary and negotiator. How fun does that sound? The internal complaints department? No, thank you . . .

I was losing hope of finding something I liked when Angela Ahrendts, then executive vice president of Liz Claiborne, called me. In 2003 the Liz Claiborne Group had acquired Juicy Couture, still a superstar casual-wear phenomenon, and now they wanted to launch its first fragrance and needed a consultant beauty expert to help.

I'm not sure if it's because Pam (Skaist-Levy) and Gela (Nash-Taylor), the founders of Juicy Couture, are slightly bonkers like me, but when it came to guidance for their new fragrance, Angela thought I'd be a good fit. For me, it was a dream assignment. The girls are a riot – I knew this from our dealings at Henri Bendel. After years in beauty retail telling brands what to do, I would finally have a hand in the creative execution of a product, from beginning to end. Plus, it meant I got to hop to and from Los Angeles, enjoying a few poolside martinis between meetings.

Juicy Couture at this point was a whole other beast to the one I'd first launched in Henri Bendel several years ago. It had transformed itself into a global brand worn by celebrities, with flagships selling not only clothing, but handbags, shoes and accessories. In addition, it was now owned by one of the biggest apparel retail groups in the US. The girls, Pam and Gela – feisty, funny, always decked out in dramatic garb and headpieces – had become celebrities in their own right and TV sound-bite candy. Juicy Couture was on a roll.

To watch Pam and Gela's interviews is sometimes misleading because their Los Angeles exuberance and eccentricity, their tans, not to mention the fun spirit of the brand, distracts from the fact that these women are extremely savvy. They had razor-sharp vision when it came to their business and always knew exactly what they wanted. It was the same when we started discussing their fragrance (just try to stand in the way of those girls – I dare you). We worked together to temper the fragrance concept into something that was commercial, but still in keeping with the brand.

Creating Juicy Couture's debut signature scent was like being in a candy shop for me. From the packaging, to the notes, to the concept, it was terrific fun to phone up producers and get hoards of crazy samples sent over. Plus, Juicy lent itself to something a bit more playful, so we didn't necessarily need to stick to the usual rules of classic fragrance launches.

The girls were after 'Big Floral', but these can be tricky to get right. One big note too far and it's an eighties Giorgio rebirth. It needs to be sophisticated. The in-house fragrance team at Liz Claiborne, the girls and I looked at ingredients and notes we liked; we then put the brief out to a few established traditional scent makers and innovators to create samples. From there we selected the manufacturer we wanted to work with and a nose. We ended up choosing Harry Fremont, at Firmenich (creator of CK One, just one of the blockbusters on his résumé). Meanwhile, we got to work on the packaging, bottle design and marketing strategy.

It still makes me laugh when people developing huge commercial fragrance lines say to me: 'We've got to get the fragrance right first!' Fragrance is the *last* thing. You've got to get the marketing story, then the bottle, then the packaging. Only then do you fill it up. It sounds cynical, but it's true with the big blockbusters.

The girls had found in a flea market a liquor bottle that they loved and wanted to use as a reference for the bottle shape. In the finished design, this translated into a chunky square glass bottle with a thick weighted bottom and angular glass stopper. The bottle is finished with a silver padlock and key, and an embossed silver Juicy Couture metal label is attached to the front, just like an old-fashioned liquor bottle, except with Juicy's two Highland Terriers on it. The scent, for the record, ended up as a big, yet sophisticated floral, with top notes of watermelon, mandarin, passion fruit, and a heart of tuberose and lily. It was an instant smash when it launched in the US in 2006, winning FiFi Fragrance of the Year.

Even today, one of my retirement venture ideas is to launch a fragrance. I loved working on that scent. For now, Liberty of London's beauty department is one of the leading hubs for independent, niche, groundbreaking and beautiful fragrances.

It was somewhere during the toing and froing on Juicy Couture's fragrance that I heard about a job coming up at Bergdorf Goodman. News hit that Muriel Gonzalez had left the store to join Ann Taylor Stores Corp. and they were looking for someone to join, taking over as senior vice president and general merchandise manager for footwear, cosmetics, fine and fashion jewellery, handbags and soft accessories.

It was a big job, and the pinnacle as far as working in luxury retail goes – major responsibility, working for the jewel in the crown of New York stores. I wanted it.

There are luxury stores, and then there are luxury stores in Manhattan – but none hold the real cachet, or mythic status, that Bergdorf Goodman does in the New York shopping landscape. It's partly down to the location: the grand stone building, built in 1928, flanks the Plaza, occupies a whole block of Fifth Avenue and overlooks the corner of Central Park. Founded in 1899 by Herman Bergdorf, then owned and managed by entrepreneur Edwin Goodman, and later his son Andrew Goodman, it is a New York institution immortalized in countless movies, television shows and novels as the place celebrities, socialites and millionaire heiresses shopped. In 2013 it was granted its very own feature-length documentary movie: *Scatter my Ashes at Bergdorf's*.

While everyone from aspirational twenty-somethings to businesswomen shop at Bloomingdale's or Barneys in New York, the rich establishment shop at Bergdorf Goodman, for everything from shoes and handbags to furs and diamonds. As such, it's always had a sense of refinement and polish. The service is second to none: little wonder when a good Bergdorf salesperson can make six figures. Meanwhile, everything from the finish of the skirting boards to the window displays is slick and beautifully executed. Bergdorf Goodman's windows are famous in their own right, and draw a crowd every time they are changed. Their mastermind is David Hoey, a genuinely creative retail visionary.

Though Bergdorf Goodman is owned by the luxury retail group Neiman Marcus (which in turn today is owned by CPP Investment Board and Ares Management), it is very much treated as a separate and distinct business from the Neiman Marcus stores, and as a result has always retained its special New Yorkerishness – for want of a more eloquent description. It is a New York landmark. This is helped by the fact that, save for the odd abandoned foray, Bergdorf Goodman has never expanded into regional stores. It is a singular business. In the 1990s, the womenswear sales grew so big that the whole store was devoted to women's goods, with menswear opening in its own store across the street (occupying the former FAO Schwarz toystore building, the setting of the famous piano scene in *Big*, starring Tom Hanks). But you will only find Bergdorf Goodman on Fifth Avenue in New York.

Unlike floundering rivals such as Bonwit Teller & Co. which had vanished by the turn of the new millennium, Bergdorf Goodman has managed to evolve with the times. In the eighties, the wealthy carriage trade who had always made it their first stop started to fall off, and it was Bergdorf Goodman's famous president, Dawn Mello, who ensured the conservative store kept relevant with new

At the Acne Studios x Liberty collaboration party with the fabulous John Sizzle.

The queue around the Liberty store for the Best of British Open Call, filmed for the TV series *Britain's Next Big Thing* in 2011. People came from as far as Australia to take part!

Above: The Best of British Open Call 2014, with Channel 4 filming.

Right: It's not all glamour! Proof that I do go white-water rafting.

Left: At the Liberty Christmas window reveal in 2014 with Judy Rose and Liz, who both featured in the TV show.

The promotional image for Channel 4's documentary, *Liberty of London*.

Above left: The Richard E. Grant perfume launch.

Above: Dita Von Teese and some dapper gents outside Liberty.

Left: With Pharrell Williams at his perfume launch.

design talent and labels in the seventies and eighties. Mello, another doyenne, holds a legendary status in retail and fashion history and is a Bergdorf Goodman icon. In 1975, she famously spotted Michael Kors decorating the window of a store called Lothar's opposite Bergdorf's, quickly plucking him from obscurity to create his own line. She also hired then-rising New York designer Tom Ford – who later became creative director of Gucci. Mello worked for Bergdorf Goodman from 1975 to 1989; for Gucci between 1989 and 1994; and returned to Bergdorf Goodman until 1999 to resume her post with additional responsibility for creative direction of the store.

In 2004 – the year I left Henri Bendel – Mello was long gone from Bergdorf Goodman. Robert Burke had taken over as fashion director. The now-famous Linda Fargo was creative director of special projects and windows. The store had also recently benefited from a large, lavish restoration over two years, with new standalone designer boutiques added for Chanel, Gucci and Versace on the upper floors.

At this juncture, Bergdorf Goodman was at the forefront of New York retail, but image-wise it had fallen slightly behind the grooviness of Barneys. Barneys, slightly north of Bergdorf's on Madison Avenue, had become the cutting-edge store in the early noughties, famed for stocking hot new talents thanks to the vision of its then-fashion director, Julie Gilhart. Gilhart was early to spot Proenza Schouler, Balenciaga and a host of other rising labels. Throughout that first decade of the new millennium, Barneys would give Bergdorf Goodman a run for its money in ready-to-wear.

To me, then, Bergdorf Goodman was an elusive, glamorous dream date who had expressed vague interest but persistently pushed me away. I'd been there for several interviews, and second interviews, but never made it into the inner sanctum. So I was surprised when this time, for the massive role of senior vice president and general merchandiser at the store, I got a call back from Jim Gold, then the president and CEO of Bergdorf Goodman.

Gold was travelling a lot at the time and we kept struggling to meet, but then he mentioned out of the blue one day that he was going home to Scarsdale for the weekend. It was as though luck sent a little fairy dust my way. 'Scarsdale!' I exclaimed quickly. 'That's the town right next to my hometown, Crestwood!' It also happened I was going back for a barbecue that weekend, a fact that I enthusiastically reported to Jim. Before I knew where I was, I was being asked over to meet with him for coffee and banana bread on the Friday evening.

Showing up for what might be one of the most important job interviews of your life at someone's home is surreal to say the least. What do you bring? What do you wear? An especially tricky decision on a humid New York evening in late summer. Eventually I chose to take my CV, and to wear a smart, crisp white shirt and blazer. Nervously, I sped over in my hire car, taking a deep breath as I pressed the doorbell at his manicured house, with sprinklers either side and neat flower beds lining the path. It became more unnerving when Beth, one of the former assistant buyers at Henri Bendel, opened the front door – she, it transpired, was also Jim's wife. All that time at Henri Bendel she had never mentioned it, ever the professional. She brought me back into the kitchen and poured me coffee. Jokingly, I berated her for not letting on she was married to one of the most powerful men in retail.

When I eventually sat down in his living room that evening, the whole meeting with Jim had an air of fate about it. Despite being hugely important, Jim has a disarming relaxed manner about him: he is tall, with jet-black hair and a Texan lilt. He was also remarkably young to be so successful, but that's because he's a consummate merchant (he has since risen to chief merchandising officer and president of the Neiman Marcus Group).

Jim and I really hit it off right away and chatted for a long time about my plans, what I would do in the role and for the company. It was the first time that I could see my Bergdorf Goodman dream finally becoming reality. Little did I know that it would be another six months, and a few touch-and-go moments, before I got the final job offer. Neiman Marcus, the parent company of Bergdorf Goodman, will not be rushed by anyone.

First, I was flown to the company's Dallas headquarters. There I met Burton Tansky, the legendary CEO of the Neiman Marcus Group (now vice chairman of Marvin Traub's consultancy). The meeting was going well until Burt pulled me to one side to pass on his own rules for Bergdorf Goodman, should I take over. At the time, the store had its beauty floor in the basement, which was visible from the ground floor thanks to a large circular cut-out balcony. The designer brands – the Guccis, Chanels and Yves Saint Laurents – were grouped together as 'super brand' boutiques on the first floor. These housed ready-to-wear and bags in separate contained units.

Both of these arrangements seemed to me to present opportunities. The circular cut-out on the ground floor ate into the most valuable retail space. Meanwhile, bags had become a bonanza luxury category in recent years, a must-have item not only for regular, seasoned luxury shoppers, but also to middle-income girls in search of an aspirational investment piece. To place a label's entire collection on the first floor ignored the fact that you were trying to attract two slightly different consumers. Accessories were a common denominator, but ready-to-wear was more exclusive. The ground floor, with its buzz and constant traffic, was the perfect place to sell handbags.

I was ready to boast about my strategy when Burt turned to me and said: 'Whatever you do at Bergdorf Goodman, don't cover up that hole which shows customers the beauty floor. People will never find the beauty department! Oh, and don't think you're bringing handbags to the ground floor, either.' My heart sank, though I got my way eventually when they gave me the job. But such an early disconnect in strategy was a little unnerving, to say the least.

Then there was the global head of human resources. While everyone I had met up until that point had been faintly amused by my offbeat activities at Henri Bendel, she was concerned. Could I really transition from hosting RuPaul parties and naked men in bathtubs to overseeing a sophisticated store and millions of dollars of their business at Bergdorf Goodman? She needed some convincing.

Jim delivered the news gently: 'It's been suggested I see other candidates,' he said after I left Texas . . . Thud . . . But then, months later he called me back, saying that he'd seen other people but wanted to see me again.

I felt emboldened; they had to like something about me. Rather than let anyone point out my shortcomings for the post, I was upfront about them, confessing every major weakness. I'd never bought footwear, for example, which was a huge part of Bergdorf Goodman's business. The difference in scale between Bergdorf Goodman's business and Henri Bendel's was obvious – but then so was my success at Bendel's.

Many more meetings followed and then, half a year after banana bread in Jim's kitchen, I found myself seated across from him in the restaurant of Bergdorf Goodman's men's store on Fifth Avenue. It was midday, June, and one of those glorious sun-covered days in New York where every colour seems saturated. There were starched tablecloths, and waiters buzzed around the air-conditioned confines of the room. I knew Jim well enough by now to guess that if he wasn't going to give me the job, he would not have suggested meeting in person. But still, it didn't seem locked in. Then the words came. 'We'd like to give you the job.'

I breathed out. After six months of waiting, I'd made it. Senior vice president and general merchandise manager, overseeing Bergdorf Goodman's fastest-growing, highest-margin businesses: footwear, cosmetics, fine and fashion jewellery, handbags and soft accessories. It was agreed that I would start on 5 July 2005.

'It's the Good Housekeeping Seal of Approval!' trilled Scott on the phone as I walked slowly down the street afterwards. 'You're official now.'

It sounds trite but that is actually exactly how I felt. I'd loved working at Henri Bendel, but it was small fry in comparison – the Chanel business alone at Bergdorf Goodman was relatable to Henri Bendel's entire turnover. This was big league, and that big league was recognizing me.

A part of me also knew I *needed* that job. I could continue running projects of a similar size to Henri Bendel, but then I would never truly know how to operate at the top tier of retail business, and at that scale. My time at Bergdorf Goodman, like Bloomingdale's, turned out to be new and challenging, but transformative. Now I just had to prove I could handle it.

The pressure was not lost on me. On my first day, as I introduced myself to everyone, it immediately became clear that the suit I had chosen would need to be upgraded. Bergdorf's dress code, like its bottom line, was serious and non-negotiable. Suits must be worn. Ditto, pocket squares. Shoes must be shined, at all times.

I embarked right away on what, to this day, is my most extravagant shopping spree (think Julia Roberts in *Pretty Woman*, with a moustache, and you'll get close). Coached by Scott, I hit every designer store in Manhattan, gathering up armfuls of shirts, coordinating ties and accessories along the way. We hit Barneys, then Prada, then Gucci, then Jeffrey – bizarrely, nothing would fit me in Bergdorf Goodman. I worked it out afterwards: in that makeover, my wardrobe alone amounted to $25,000.

The new wardrobe was worth it, though. My favourite was a grey flannel Jil Sander suit that I wore so much it eventually split while I was picking something up off the sidewalk. Not a tiny rip – a giant, gaping flap. I was on a buying trip in Paris. Thank God Scott was there. I had to shuffle back to the hotel with him two feet behind, walking Marx Brothers style. I will never forget the image of Scott and I in tandem. That's what friends are for.

I also changed my demeanour during this time, though not to my friends. I've always focused on being nice – uniformly, to everyone – and I retained this, but Bergdorf Goodman's style was altogether more formal and conservative. Like my buttoned-up suit, I buttoned up at Bergdorf's. It was helped in some ways by having zero personal life. Working in a role as prominent as that takes over your existence.

I found that exercise helped. I've always been a swimming addict, but I also started working out three times a week with a personal trainer. I've come to realize that New York personal trainers are unlike any other trainers in the world – in that they beat the shit out of you. My taskmaster was David Kirsch, at the time one of the hottest (not to mention most expensive) trainers in the city. Kirsch's gyms are famed for their privacy. Only two people can work out, maximum, at the same time, and they're kept separate – which is a good thing because you look so sweaty you think you're going to die (not so Heidi Klum, though, who glistened with unnatural beauty during her workouts when she was there). Most of the fashion magazine editors went to Kirsch because of his discretion. I remember rolling over, purple-faced and out of breath on a mat once, to face a famous beauty magazine editor, similarly purple and sweaty. There we were, face-to-face in our least glamorous states. Without blinking she quipped: 'If you tell anyone about this, I. Will. Kill. You.'

***

I did find escape at this time though. For years I'd been visiting Montauk, which at that point was the least fashionable, undiscovered far end of Long Island. It was the antithesis of the glitzy Hamptons or party-centric Fire Island, with rustic windswept beaches. I'd started renting a small, seventies wood-clad beach shack while I was at Henri Bendel, and I'd fallen in love with the place. It was a couple of blocks from the beach, and from the outside it looked unremarkable. It had giant windows on both sides of the building, meaning that light swam in throughout the day. As the pressure of my career increased, this shack became my haven. By the time I was at Bergdorf Goodman, I was able to buy it (that is, after I'd paid the bill from the shopping spree). I started lining it with antiques, Jean Cocteau line drawings and paintings I'd collected over the years. I still have the house, though Montauk itself has since been discovered by New York money and ruined with glossy restaurants and boutiques. I've started to rent it out in summers because it is overrun, but I still regularly visit in winter, when it's totally dead. That's just the way I like it: it's a bit like *The Shining*. In winter, mine is the only light on the beach and there are no street lights – nothing beats it for blissful solitude and time to clear your mind. The beaches in the crisp winter sun are like nothing else.

Then there are the hurricanes. In the height of summer, with the gentle whoosh of the waves in the background, you can happily sleep on the beach in Montauk. On those evenings it's difficult to imagine the storm-ravaged scenes that occur: they can be quite terrifying, partly because you feel like you're on the tip of the world (actually, the tip of Long Island). Winds swirl around and batter the wooden-clad houses, which emit sinister creaks. The strange thing about hurricanes in Montauk is that after the storm has passed, the beaches are swept entirely clean. All the debris has been whisked off somewhere else. The sea becomes like a still, glacial pond. It's completely surreal. In fact, the weather in general is why I like Montauk: the brisk winters, the windy afternoons, the hurricanes. I love the incredible winter fog we get there – a mystic blanket of dampness that creeps over everything. When you come inside from a five-minute walk on the beach, you see that every hair follicle on your face is coated in droplets of water.

***

When I joined Bergdorf Goodman, its women's business (the menswear store, across the street, was treated as a separate business) generated about $550 million in revenue – roughly twelve times that of Henri Bendel. The senior vice presidency was split between myself and Ginny Hershey-Lambert. Essentially, Ginny controlled everything that had a sleeve; I controlled the rest.

Together, we ran the show, with our vice presidents covering specific categories from shoes, to bags, to jewellery, and with senior buyers and buying teams below them. Under me, I had vice presidents Deborah Soss who worked on accessories and bags; Sally Ross who bought footwear (and who was later joined by Scott Tepper); Sydney Price who bought jewellery; and Pat Saxby who oversaw beauty. All were seasoned experts.

Ginny, my counterpart, was another Texan. She'd transferred from Neiman's Dallas headquarters where she bought couture collections. In a way, she reminded me of Sharon from the days at Bonwit Teller & Co. I knew the second I met her that I'd like Ginny. She had dark hair, pale skin and a great, wide smile. I asked her on my first day to give me the lowdown on the personalities at Bergdorf Goodman (of which there are many) and her descriptions – humorous, affectionate, but candid – revealed everything I needed to know about both her and the staff.

Elevated turnover means elevated stakes. There are no 'oops' moments if you make a mistake: it could cost the company millions. Vendor relationships were crucial. Chanel, Dior, Gucci, Prada and all the other blue-chip brands amounted to a huge chunk of the business, which meant I had to maintain close, near symbiotic relationships with the managers. If product was going anywhere first, it was going to Bergdorf Goodman.

Fashion weeks were also different. As president of Henri Bendel, visiting Paris or Milan Fashion Week was – in comparison – a Roman holiday involving shows, a few appointments, some dinners and meetings and an espresso here and there. It was all relatively relaxed and convivial. Not so at Bergdorf Goodman. Arriving en masse in Paris or Milan was planned with precision; every moment of your time was accounted for. From the second the jet landed it was like a military operation, a touchdown by the US luxury retail marines. We scattered, searched, and negotiated.

Meetings were also on another level. Bergdorf Goodman largely carries only successful labels. Every inch of space was covered by major brands, all of which could comfortably earn their keep. Forget a relaxed espresso and looking through the rails in a showroom. Everything was boardroom level in terms of scale of importance. You'd be sitting there in a grand office around a giant table, with Dior's chiefs, Domenico Dolce and Stefano Gabbana, or Tod's CEO Diego Della Valle, explaining what worked in collections, what didn't, what they needed to improve on.

There were sometimes tough conversations. Back then, shoes and accessories were the cash cow for every luxury brand and so even fine jewellery houses were adding new handbag lines to their offer, but not everyone was successful. Often big brands which had a big ready-to-wear business with us would try to lean in on retailers, forcing them to buy the shoes or the bags when they were introduced – even if they were junk. But we had to tactfully explain, to a table of twelve people, why we didn't want them.

I remember one CEO for a major luxury brand exclaiming to me: 'Tell me *why*! Why will you not buy them?' And you could never say: 'Actually, because the colours are terrible and they're gratuitously overpriced.' It was a delicate negotiation of ego and a masterclass in disaster diffusion. We needed them onside, after all, for other categories of our business.

I also had to learn the Bergdorf Goodman (and Neiman Marcus) approach to travel expenses. At Henri Bendel I'd tip waiters, get my clothes laundered and pressed when I arrived, have breakfast at the hotel, and generally not even think twice about buying dinner. I remember turning in my first Bergdorf's expense sheet after a trip to Europe, in which I'd also signed for laundering my entire suitcase of clothes at the Ritz Hotel in Paris. Jim Gold came back to me with the report, covered in yellow sticky notes with question marks: 'Never. In my life. Have I seen anything like this, Ed!' He had a point: the Ritz Laundry alone was eye-wateringly expensive. I bought my own coffees in future.

Despite the insane schedules, I did get some spare time in Paris. From my Henri Bendel buying trips onwards, I'd discovered Clignancourt, or *Les Puces* ('The Fleas'), a vast antiques market on the outskirts of the city. It's fair to say Clignancourt is in quite a shabby area – the last place you'd expect to find treasures such as rare antiques and vintage fashion, but it's all there, housed in a small 'village' of low-rise garages, stalls and emporia. This was where I really started collecting in earnest. The French traders hated me at first, of course – the brash American – but once I started buying anything from antique chairs to Chanel tables and mirrors, African masks to Indonesian bed frames, they changed their tune. Pretty soon, I would only need to walk in and they'd hand me a purchase book. I'd simply put dots on everything I liked and they'd load it up into giant shipping containers.

I developed an insatiable appetite for buying incredible, beautiful things. I'd see something amazing and have to have it, even if it was totally impractical. Once I bought a Balinese table so big that when it was finally delivered to my apartment – several floors up – in New York, the deliverymen refused to carry it up. Plus, I had totally misjudged my measurements; there was no way it was even going to fit in my apartment, or through the front door for that matter. I had to turn to them, and other curious onlookers on the sidewalk, and say: 'So do any of *you* want this? It's yours if you do!'

I have had to learn not to get too attached and to remind myself that these things are – at the end of the day – just things. Tragedy struck a few years ago. I'd stored a lot of my collection in my Montauk house, which was then flooded, ruining everything there. The insurers didn't know what to do either. They had to get a specialist in to value some of the rarer items. It was very traumatic for me to lose a lifetime of trinkets I'd found, but I focused on the fact that I have my friends and family. Plus, it's given me an excuse to buy more . . .

My office at Bergdorf Goodman was on the executive floor. I was in one corner. Ginny was in the other. We flanked Robert Burke, vice president of fashion and public relations. My office was directly under Bergdorf Goodman's John Barrett beauty salon, which was on the ninth floor (the former residence of the Goodman family). My office was great, except for the fact that I was right beneath the pedicure tubs, which frequently leaked, and sometimes collapsed. I was in a constant state of red alert, ready for action should the ceiling cave in.

Robert Burke left very soon after I joined to set up his own luxury and retail consultancy. He was, even then, entrepreneurial. He was always impeccably dressed and unfailingly professional, and also very good for a sound bite.

Robert recommended promoting Linda Fargo as his successor when he left Bergdorf Goodman, putting in place what is now one of Bergdorf's major figureheads. Raised in Midwest America, Linda is a worker. She'd worked her way up in retail, spending time in San Francisco working for Gap before becoming creative director of windows at Bergdorf Goodman. At the time, this new role was a great step up for her, but it's since led to amazing things. Linda has become a major figurehead for the store, and a style icon of Bergdorf Goodman, known for her sleek white bob and striking dress style.

What I have always loved about Linda is that she is a true gatekeeper of the store's excellence. Everything at Bergdorf Goodman is slightly elevated and slicker than other players. This is part of its DNA. Sometimes, as departments move through different sets of hands, this can slip, but Linda has always defended it – fiercely. I remember being in meetings with her to discuss proposals for a new department or event and she'd come back, quick as a flash, with cost-per-square-footage (usually way higher than the creative had estimated). But her policy was that no garbage was ever going on the shop floor. No mediocrity at Bergdorf Goodman, thank you.

I also got to know Jim Gold well while working with him. Our offices were on the same floor. He was a very inspirational colleague. He saw that I understood the importance of novelty, and selecting the right pieces to get us press, but he also supported me in getting a hold on the scale of Bergdorf Goodman's numbers, which in the early days were beyond anything I'd handled before. The biggest thing I learned from Jim, though, was focus. He has a terrific sense of humour, but in the boardroom it is 100 per cent about the business. How do we resolve this issue? How do we improve this? What do we need? He is never unduly harsh. He delivers feedback in a direct, efficient manner, but it is never political or loaded with any agenda. Like Angela Ahrendts and Ted Marlow, who I have also taken great inspiration from in my career, Jim Gold's priority is singular: get the job done, and do it brilliantly. Every decision stems from this endeavour. So, while working for him is demanding, and there is pressure, there is never the sense of emotional anxiety that comes with juggling a 'personality'. I found this then, and continue to find it now, a brilliant way to work. It simplifies everything and you get the best out of people because there's no fear of over-thinking issues.

There was a sense of true professionalism that I really enjoyed while at Bergdorf Goodman. It's the kind of thing you see at any established company at the pinnacle of its field. Everyone there had done their time and was there for one simple reason: they were good, *very* good. It was all about getting on, and continually delivering. In this sense, while pressured, it was cyclical, like a big industrial machine. If you could keep fuelling the giant, diamond-encrusted engine, you were fine.

Though, in working for a machine, you were also always aware that you were just one cog. While at Henri Bendel I could have ordered a strippergram dressed like Arnold Schwarzenegger to conduct a live nude-painting illustration while playing ping-pong – if I wanted. By contrast, everything was decided by committee at Bergdorf's.

But, by 2006, Bergdorf Goodman did need to take some risks. While no one could touch it for accessories, jewellery and shoes, our ready-to-wear was slightly behind the curve. Barneys had scooped up what would come to be the most important new wave of European talent and resurging brands, from Givenchy to Dries Van Noten, to Olivier Theyskens, Azzedine Alaïa and Balenciaga, from under Bergdorf's nose.

This became painfully apparent when we held the famous seasonal Neiman Marcus and Bergdorf Goodman breakfast with *Vogue*'s editorial staff. The breakfast saw all of the Neiman Marcus and Bergdorf heads, including Burt Tansky and *Vogue*'s Anna Wintour, gathered over croissants, fruit plates and coffee at the Ritz Hotel, Paris, to discuss what collections and designers they felt had been most important that season. I remember the horror when Sally Singer, then *Vogue*'s fashion features director, delivered her recommendations and we realized we had about three of the six designers. Afterwards, it prompted a huddle of panicked whispers, as the company formed a new strategy to seize some of these talents. We knew we needed to redress the balance – quickly.

This change of tack sometimes meant stepping away from Bergdorf's famed image of untouchability. Azzedine Alaïa's ready-to-wear had been incredible for a while. We'd been selling his shoes with great success, but when it came to the suggestion of expanding to Azzedine's ready-to-wear, one Bergdorf executive batted off the suggestion: 'He's just not hungry enough to be in Bergdorf Goodman.' But Azzedine Alaïa doesn't get hungry. He's one of fashion's anomalies. He's perfectly charming when you're in business, but the fact is – such is his reputation and influence – he doesn't need to beg. Eventually, we got him on board. And, as we suspected, it was hugely successful.

Luxury was exploding when I joined Bergdorf Goodman, right up until 2008. The economy was booming and luxury brands were running with it, big time. It was an orgy of spending, in which customers seemingly had an unquenchable thirst for piles of luxury. It was almost indecent looking back on it; not to mention unsustainable.

Nowhere was this more evident than accessories. The average price of luxury bags and shoes had virtually doubled in a year, from $1,000 to $2,000, then $4,000. One handbag was not enough for any consumer; they needed a wardrobe. Plus, the fashion houses had become accustomed to adding significant hardware appendages to each design, linking it directly to a particular season – and thereby making each bag obsolete by the next seasonal drop. Pre-collections ramped up, as consumers engaged in a frenzy of accelerated and inexhaustible consumption.

Needless to say, I made sure Bergdorf Goodman cashed in. I could never understand the policy of keeping accessories with the complete collection by a brand on a higher floor. Accessories during this time had almost become like beauty, an impulse category, so despite Burt Tansky's initial advice to me, that's where I placed them: the impulse zone, on the ground floor.

We unveiled the new ground-floor accessories section in 2008: a 3,000-square-foot sanctuary, housing all the accessories categories together, marking the final stage of an extravagant eighteen-month renovation of the store. The department was spectacular, featuring Swarovski chandeliers, sleek glass cases and lavish onyx details. We brought in Goyard luggage – then the hottest thing. We brought in Azzedine Alaïa, Balenciaga and Lanvin. We also expanded a shoe salon to include every one of the new European labels we stocked. Customers were able to buy the eyewear, glasses, shoes, bags and belts from any one of their favourite designers in one spot, as well as cult accessory brands such as Pierre Hardy, Chrome Hearts and Pauric Sweeney.

Pricing was an incentive in itself: the higher the better, which made exotic accessories a key focus. Crocodile, python, ostrich, alligator – that was the easiest way to add a few zeros to a purchase. Exotic labels such as Nancy Gonzalez, famed for luxurious, brightly coloured skins, took centre stage. Meanwhile, brands hurriedly rolled out every iconic style in sumptuous skins, while playing around with more experimental exotic treatments. Fur went nuts, too. Everything came with a chinchilla trim, a fox pompom, and was rabbit-lined. Bergdorf Goodman always had a fur department. It was famous for it, but the furs were self-contained. Now fur was being introduced into every brand's collection in a rainbow of colours and treatments. (Later, for autumn 2008, Fendi developed a special technique for coating the tips of fur in real twenty-four-carat gold. Its mink gold-tipped coats sold for $64,300.) It is so refreshing that at Liberty we have a no-fur policy. It's simply not something that anyone ever needs!

Jewellery was understandably huge. The bigger the diamonds, the better. We expanded the fine jewellery department, adding to the assortment lines such as Pomellato and Lorraine Schwartz, in addition to in-store boutiques for brands such as Buccellati, Verdura and Kieselstein-Cord. Sales of fine jewellery went through the roof, and doubled in the time I was at Bergdorf Goodman.

I remember our jewellery buyer, Sydney, coming in one day during this boom exclaiming: 'The belt has sold! We sold the belt!' I was a bit shocked at her excitement over a mere belt and retorted to her as a joke: 'Er, shouldn't we be concentrating on the jewels?' Then she elaborated. It was *the* belt: a diamond and ruby encrusted fine jewellery snake belt piece by Jean Schlumberger, the world-famous fine jewellery designer and artist. It had sold for $65,000.

After that, needless to say, I encouraged her to sell as many belts as she could.

Despite the serious business at hand, there were funny moments at Bergdorf Goodman's, and funny characters. I loved Pat Saxby, our beauty buyer. We were like for like, and shared an irreverent attitude to the luxury industry. She'd call me on the phone after dramas with some of our beauty brands: 'Ed, are you there? Can I just rant at you for a while?' I obliged. Her rants were always so funny.

Then there was Betty Halbreich, the head of Bergdorf Goodman's personal shopping department. Betty is famous throughout New York – the fact that she takes centre stage in the store's documentary *Scatter my Ashes at Bergdorf's* is no surprise to me. She is exactly as she appears on camera – petite, with gamine-like grey short hair, lightning-sharp wit, and a killer death-stare. She is an absolute force, and not to be trifled with. If you didn't have the collection pieces she was after for a client, that was it; she'd march straight up to your office and tell you off. She made such a huge amount of money for the store that you listened to her, though. The best part was her facial expressions. You only needed to see the way she'd look a customer up and down in an elevator to know exactly what she was thinking. I had to stop myself cracking up sometimes, as some scruffy twenty-something stepped in, decked out in designer grey marl schlub clothes (à la Alexander Wang). She was not a fan of the 'off-duty model' look when it became a Manhattan phenomenon, and you saw every young person parading around in relaxed jersey draped T-shirts and leather jackets: Betty's look was so much more refined.

There were fun times. Every season, Neiman Marcus would host a dinner at Tong Yen, the upscale Chinese restaurant in Paris, to celebrate the end of runway season for all Bergdorf Goodman and Neiman buyers. It was one of the few moments that Bergdorf employees would get to let their hair down. While diners daintily ate from white linen-covered tables on the floors beneath, our group would have the whole top floor for a raucous drunken banquet, guzzling free booze and feasting on noodles. Speeches always punctuated the end of the evening, and often led to some amusing moments. I remember Burt Tansky, the CEO of Neiman Marcus, got up one season at the peak of the boom, exclaiming in merriment: 'Just buy what sells! And leave the rest to Saks . . .' That was it. I loved it.

Parties at Bergdorf were different to those at Henri Bendel. Everything was more restrained and conservative, which meant instead of a big flashy MAC launch, we'd have a champagne reception for a new coffee-table book, an exhibition at the Metropolitan Museum of Art, or a salon with one of the fashion designers.

Manolo Blahnik was a regular at Bergdorf Goodman events. Manolo is a character I've become close to over the years, both as a collaborator and friend. I'm proud to say that Liberty of London was the first store, outside of his own boutique, where Manolo sells his shoes. The man is creative, very sweet, endearingly eccentric and has unstoppable energy. He's in his seventies now, and yet when he does personal appearances he stays way beyond the time agreed – and they always draw massive crowds. He is also an avid pop-culture addict. I remember at one of the Bergdorf Goodman appearances, the *Buffy the Vampire Slayer* star Sarah Michelle Gellar happened to be perusing the shoe department. I rushed over to introduce her to him, thinking he'd have no idea who she was, but he was too fast: '*Buffy!*' he exclaimed, with his arms open to embrace her. It turns out that Manolo Blahnik is a big Buffy fan and was elated to have his picture taken with Sarah Michelle.

***

For my entire time at Bergdorf I ran a successful secondary shrink business named 'Ed's Sofa'. It was about being the ear, listening to woes, rants, worries and personal problems, and enabling people to continue doing their job. You sure get some crazy personalities in retail, but it doesn't matter if they're good. If they're good, they get a bonus, and you get a bonus. They're worth the investment. A lot of my job was about maintaining some form of equilibrium and calm, reassuring them that their life is going the right way, that they are talented, and that their cat wouldn't die.

It was around 2007, two years after I started at Bergdorf Goodman, that I first got a call from Liberty of London. I wasn't sure what to make of it at the time, but then Geoffroy De La Bourdonnaye, the French chief executive of the store, called me to follow up. He asked, in his deep, thick French accent, for a meeting, and as I was about to be in London for a buying trip, I agreed.

Liberty of London . . . I knew it, and of course it was one of my favourite shopping spots when I visited the city. It is a beautiful gem of a store, with amazing wooden beams and crammed with charm, but it seemed to have lost its way on recent visits. At the time, it had rather a hodgepodge of goods and had given in to its eccentricities; but it was still a national treasure.

I met with Geoffroy, a slim, smartly dressed man with slate-grey hair, and what was supposed to be a quick coffee turned into a two-hour, detailed walk through the store. I took him from top to bottom, telling him precisely what I believed was wrong, and everything I would do to rectify it. Emboldened by not being emotionally engaged, I pulled no punches, declaring as I looked at the ground-floor stationery stockrooms: 'Are you kidding me? Why are you giving prime ground-floor selling space to stationery storage?!'

Shortly after they called, and to my surprise, they offered me a position as buying director. I turned it down. The privately owned company didn't seem to have the funds I thought would be necessary to make it work again. They were also investing in an ill-fated Liberty brand, which I believed wouldn't work. It was an amicable parting, though.

Even then, after the offer, I didn't take the role at Liberty of London that seriously. I had been curious, that's all. Little did I know that they'd call again when the world was about to end in 2008, at which point I'd also become more serious, and more curious, about this funny little store in London.

The signs had been there for a while. You don't need the stock-market results, really. Economists should just talk to retailers for early signs of a crisis. We saw it right from the start of 2008. The seemingly endless boom for luxury, which had propelled the industry into major profits as customers scooped armfuls of clothes, bags and shoes, had started to slow.

Then came the stock-market crash of September 2008. The problem for Bergdorf Goodman was that, like everybody else, we'd bought collections for autumn based on the phenomenal growth of previous seasons. We had to cancel, or dramatically reduce, our orders in many cases. I remember going to Valentino one morning around then, having ordered $800,000 worth of stock (at retail value), and telling them that I needed to cancel half. That was just the beginning.

The major crisis occurred for us in November 2008, two months after the crash. The slowdown had been happening for a while, but suddenly got worse in New York when, amid rising panic throughout the city over slow sales in the run-up to Thanksgiving, Saks Fifth Avenue suddenly slashed prices of accessories and fashion by as much as 70 per cent, way ahead of what was typical, and with discounts that would normally be reserved for the first day of January. Saks discounted far deeper, pre-emptively and more aggressively, than any retailer had done in the past, before the traditional holiday shopping season had even really begun.

The result at first was confusion among other New York retailers. What was this strategy? It had, understandably, been decided as a surprise – apart from anything else, to avoid alienating Saks's vendors. But the implications were huge. The move put pressure on all other department stores, including ours, to discount early and match their prices; it destroyed several retailers' profits, and broke many agreements on pricing and distribution with the brands in the process. On a larger scale, the resulting wave of heavy discounting would also transform consumer attitudes to luxury spending.

I remember walking past the signs with my jaw dropping: Valentino, down 70 per cent from $3,000; jackets originally pitched at $3,000, on sale for $900.

Under pressure, many retailers began accelerating their markdown strategy. We typically had prescribed dates for markdowns. First 20 per cent, then 40 per cent, and so on, with a clear plan in the lead up to Christmas. But all of these were brought forward. By Thanksgiving, Neiman Marcus was also promoting discounts of 50 to 65 per cent off fall and holiday goods. In previous years, those markdowns would be reserved until after Christmas.

It can't all be blamed on Saks Fifth Avenue. Other retailers had started discounting, albeit not as significantly. Behind closed doors, all sorts of sample sales and private shopping events with slashed prices were being held. Saks Fifth Avenue simply opened the floodgates.

I remember this creating a wave of spy-like paranoia among New York retailers. Our stores – Saks Fifth Avenue, Barneys and Bergdorf Goodman – were relatively close, and every morning, everyone would be checking out the others' new discount signs.

One of the biggest fallouts from the 2008 stock-market crash and subsequent crisis was the loss of smaller independent stores. While department stores cut staff, the size of collections, and costs, the strain of competing in this climate was too much for some small businesses, as it sat outside their business model. As a result, some of New York and Los Angeles's most respected boutiques shuttered in the wake. Linda Dresner, the famous owner of eponymous boutiques on Park Avenue and in Michigan, was forced to shut her Park Avenue store. Dresner's minimalist boutique in New York was famous for its edit of directional designers such as Comme des Garçons and Jil Sander, and had been there for decades. Georgina, two long-standing boutiques in Manhasset and Hewlett owned by Christina Makowsky, was also shut. Tracey Ross, the famed boutique owner in Los Angeles, also shut her store.

One such owner, Intermix co-founder Khajak Keledjian, summed up the mood in *Women's Wear Daily*:

They are rolling out insanely competitive incentives in reaction to the financial climate. The whole fashion sense and appeal is gone. It has completely ruined the season, with incentive points, offers of no interest for one year, markdowns on new merchandise that's not even two weeks old, and basically 70 per cent discounts from original prices. They are wiping out specialty retailers and young designers.

The biggest impact of the global economic crisis on luxury retail was psychological. It took years to claw back credibility. Luxury brands which had been hiking prices for some time were suddenly caught with their pants down.

Meanwhile, consumers were looking at themselves with fresh eyes, never to have the veil returned. Did I really buy this piece-of-crap bag for $3,000? Really? It was a wake-up call. No one trusted full price any more. At the same time, there was a genuine reappraisal of luxury. It suddenly became chic to be thrifty, or to wear clothes that were a few seasons old. Magazines started running features on how to 'shop your closet'.

Where people did buy luxury, there was a new sense of discretion. Bling, and obvious visual opulence was out as an aesthetic. People became secretive about their purchases, requesting goods to be shipped to their home address rather than to emerge from a store with bags of luxury merchandise. I even remember Hermès offering discreet consumers brown, plain, paper bags instead of their bright orange, logo-emblazoned ones. The whole boom in luxury spending was now seen as horribly gauche and if you did still have money, you didn't want to be seen to be the only pig on the block.

There were also thousands of individual casualties from this economic nuclear disaster. We received a wave of returns at the store as people, sometimes desperate, attempted to claw back their assets. Sales staff could be heard saying to customers: 'Madam, how many seasons ago did you buy this?' If it was a loyal customer, sometimes we'd let them return it, even if the item was too old. You learn these things with regular customers: a small act of diplomacy and trust can pay dividends later.

It was at the peak of this crisis that I received another unexpected call from Liberty. 'We haven't stopped wanting you for this job,' said Geoffroy, his French accent crackling on the phone from rainy London. He listed the improvements that Liberty had recently been making, many such changes being in line with those I'd recommended on our walkabout over a year and a half earlier.

By this point, a long period of economic malaise was on the horizon in the US. London was still buoyant, thanks to international millionaire residents and being a key international financial market.

I had also become well versed in the Bergdorf Goodman machine. I had achieved what I'd set out to – the ground-floor accessories department, filling in the beauty hole . . . I'd learned most of what I needed to. I'd even, though I hadn't realized it, fallen into a holding pattern. Bergdorf Goodman is in the big league of retail but it is a large machine, and while I loved operating at that level, I began craving the type of role where I could have more control, and more of an impact.

But did I really want to move to London? At least London, of the European capitals, was my favourite. Milan was ugly but the food and the people were terrific; still, after forty-eight hours, you've seen enough. Paris was stunning but the people always seemed difficult to me, for no reason (maybe it's my bad French!). I'd been coming to London for twenty years. I loved the energy, the fashion scene, the stores and its eccentricities.

Then it hit me. I was staring down the barrel of fifty. I was stuck in a very sparkly but repetitive rut, and wanted to be outside my comfort zone again. Rainy old England might be just the ticket.

I called Angela Ahrendts, who by then was the established CEO at Burberry in London, for advice. 'Do it,' she said emphatically, quickly giving me advice on London's best neighbourhoods. That was the affirmation I needed. I explained to Jim that it was time to move on, handed in my resignation, accepted the job of buying director, and bought a plane ticket, London-bound for my next adventure.

CHAPTER 6

LONDON CALLING: LIBERTY

It's difficult to convey exactly how I felt as I pushed my luggage cart through arrivals at London Heathrow in December 2008. I stepped outside 'Nothing to Declare', and all of a sudden it hit me like a wall.

Fear set in. What had I done? Quit my nice high-powered job in New York sitting at the top of the luxury retail food chain, Bergdorf Goodman, that's what. And for a creaking antique vessel stuffed with paisley trinkets!

I was fifty. I had my nice life in New York with my nice apartment, my beloved Montauk beach house, and I'd decided to ditch it all to live in a foreign country during what was supposed to be the golden cruise control period of my life. I was supposed to be brunching at the beach on weekends, not trying to find an apartment and master the Tube in a new city.

The cold struck as the doors parted and I made my way to the airport taxi line. A wall of bracing frost hit my face like a train. December had descended on London, and a bleak, grey mist was everywhere. London cold, I've since learned, is not like New York cold. New York can be freezing, doubtless, and way more so than

London, but it's usually a bright and crisp kind of cold. There's optimism, even in the depths of winter, to the quality of the light. London's winters are less extreme, but the winter has a damp, grey quality that seeps into your bones. And here it was, in all its dampness, to welcome me.

As the black cab driver made his way on to the motorway towards London, my rational self took over. I knew why I'd taken this job, in my heart. To begin with, I needed a new challenge. Mastering the machine that was Bergdorf Goodman was tough at first, but I'd since learned how to run it smoothly and I'd slipped into a treadmill pattern: a punishing, fast-paced treadmill pattern, but a treadmill nonetheless.

I was also still single. Twenty-five years of being a workaholic had been my making, and saved me in many ways, but for the last decade it had meant being largely alone, which is not to say that I came to London in search of my saviour millionaire husband (though that would be nice!), but if you're going to place your career at the centre of your life, you may as well keep it interesting. New York was so familiar. I'd been living in the city my entire adult life and the time was ripe for some excitement and new challenges.

In addition, something about Liberty of London had also struck a chord with me, something I'd not felt since taking charge at Henri Bendel. Looking back, I'd never been as exhilarated as when I was at the helm at Henri Bendel. It was the challenge of taking something that was small and charming, but slightly broken, and turning it around: problem-solving, my favourite. And again, with limited resources. I've always loved an underdog, and here I was being greeted with a pretty special one at that.

It was a while before I would have complete control of the

Liberty of London store – that's when the fun really started – but along the way, this foggy, cold, wet city would win me over. Liberty of London, a project, would become an all-encompassing, ongoing challenge and love affair. Its people, meanwhile, would become my good friends. I'd even get Scott to hop the pond and move in next door, when he left Bergdorf Goodman.

***

Liberty of London occupies a precious spot in many British people's hearts. In fact, anyone who visits tends to fall in love with its nooks, crevices, and majestic wooden beams. It is a lovable store, plain and simple. The 1920s Tudor-revival wooden building, with intricately carved wooden panels and a golden ship weathervane on its roof, is a London landmark; even the metal drainpipes feature ornamental detail.

It's the place where grandmothers buy gifts and knitting yarn; where decorators come for unique homewares, rugs and lamps; the place sewing and haberdashery fans come to buy beautiful British Liberty-print fabric; where mothers and daughters come to buy Christmas baubles and have tea. Shopping here is a British rite of passage. The wooden staircases creak, the basement floods, the elevators take eons to move, and the Arts and Crafts design keeps the light from reaching giant corners of the building, but everyone forgives it because it has, in spades, one thing that the other London department stores don't: charm.

Liberty of London oozes charm. It has always been the place to buy something special, and different. Customers get lost in it. They come in December simply to browse its corners and corridors for new gifts, beautiful costume jewellery, hand-printed stationery, and hard-to-find fashion labels. Or to fight it out with the crowds in our Christmas shop, which from November onwards is deluged with shoppers in search of baubles and tree ornaments. (We order 50,000 extra items of stock specifically for the Christmas shop each year.)

In 2008, Liberty still had all that charm, but you got the impression it had taken it for granted or, at least, assumed it could survive on charm alone. It couldn't. Not when its competitors were sprinting ahead.

London's luxury retail scene at this time – unlike New York's – was buoyant. New York may have been licking its wounds and adjusting to a sombre life, post-global economic crisis, but in London business was brisk. For years, London's luxury market has been an oasis in the financial meltdown, propped up by money from Russian émigrés, Middle Eastern and Chinese tourists, French, Italian and Greek residents escaping Eurozone taxes and uncertainty.

But in 2008, Liberty was seeing none of this cash. Its then-owners, the British property group Marylebone Warwick Balfour (MWB), had appointed ex-Christian Lacroix executive Geoffroy De La Bourdonnaye as CEO in 2007, with plans to revive its fortunes.

This was where I came in. The big year for Liberty's 'Renaissance' under Geoffroy was to be 2009, and I'd been drafted in to lead the key buying changes: overhauling the store edit, modernizing its offer and making it commercial once more. The plans were to unveil a renovated store in the New Year; a souped-up womenswear offer; a bazaar of accessories and jewellery; to expand its own Liberty of London luxury brand; and again to become relevant.

I looked at the sales figures and was bemused. On the surface, Liberty was successful and certainly much-loved, but for almost a decade it had been in a rut. It was flatlining. This would be fine, except that the rest of London's luxury retail scene was enjoying substantial growth. In one of the biggest run-ups in London retail, the great ship Liberty was taking on water. Alarmingly, during the first month of my arrival, we'd even struggled to make payroll. I took that sales figure and came up with my mission – I'd double it, or die trying.

Liberty of London did eventually return to profit in 2011, but the path to this was anything but straightforward, and the 'Renaissance' took longer than envisaged. To begin with, it involved new owners (soon after I joined, Liberty was sold to BlueGem, a private equity company); it would involve a departure for Geoffroy, who left to become president of Chloé; and finally, the loss of the ill-fated Liberty of London luxury brand, which had been launched in 2004.

During this time, and under new ownership, I would be promoted to managing director of the store, make my British TV debut, meet Prince Charles, and have several sleepless nights between – but it would all be worth it to revive Liberty of London's fortunes.

I celebrated that first glimpse of success in 2011 by taking my staff to dinner. I wanted to mark a small, but significant, profit but, more importantly, it was the first marker in the store's new profitable trajectory. It was also one of many moments I'd come to feel part of Liberty's 'family'. It sounds silly, but working at Liberty really is like being part of a family, with eccentric characters, moments of calamity, and many shared laughs amid the day-to-day whirring.

Since that profit in 2011, Liberty has flourished. It's been the star of a three-part documentary, which aired on Channel 4 in December 2013, bringing the magic of Liberty and its team to the homes of millions, and a second season of four episodes in

November 2014. It's seen our profits continue to rise. The British public isn't done with us yet, either.

Not that I could have foreseen any of this, as I checked into the Charlotte Street Hotel that freezing evening back in December 2008. I'd always loved Charlotte Street Hotel, and the Firmdale hotels in general. There's a hominess to their rooms – a bit like my other favourite hotel, No. 11 Cadogan Gardens in Chelsea, which feels like the setting for an episode of the classic British TV drama *Upstairs Downstairs*. Plus, Kit Kemp, the designer of Firmdale's interiors, loves a print as much as I do. That evening, Charlotte Street's cosiness and familiar panelling, overstuffed armchairs, and revellers chattering outside, provided a much-needed sense of comfort, and calm, before the storm.

The next few days were a blur of practicalities as I adjusted to life in London. First, I needed an apartment. I couldn't figure out why the estate agent kept showing me places in Marylebone, but then I realized, it's because everyone who's *not* from England lives in Marylebone. I settled on a nice big studio close to work, and that was that.

Marylebone is quite a surreal place. Save for a year living in Notting Hill, I've lived here for my entire time in London, mainly for convenience. But I've also come to appreciate its incongruity over the years. It's a funny, fake Disneyland London village, packed with historic townhouses, mews cottages and apartment blocks, populated by French, Americans, Italians, Russians – you name it – anyone but Brits. Meanwhile, its seemingly quaint high street is lined with upscale boutiques that feel like independents but are actually chains. There's your local village Waitrose . . . your local Le Pain Quotidien, your friendly White Company . . . you get the picture. For me, a service-loving, lazy American, it's the closest thing you'll get to New York ease.

I talk about this to British people and they never quite understand. There's a certain effortlessness to living in Manhattan, that – for all its charms – I've never found in the UK. Egg-white omelette to your door in torrential rain at 3 a.m.? Yup. No problem. With you in five minutes. Want your dog walker to come at thirty-minute intervals and also to collect your groceries? Fine. Dry-cleaning overnight? Not sooner? Manhattan has service culture down pat.

I recall first trying to order an internet service for my London apartment. It took three weeks to arrive, and when it did, it was just a box with a manual! No man to help me set it up, no assistance, nothing. DIY internet after three weeks?! The same thing in New York would have been delivered in twenty-four hours and personally set up by an engineer. That was the first service-culture shock of many as I got used to my new London home.

Still, at least I was close to work. Although, at first, I didn't realize how close I was to work. That's another thing I had to learn to understand in London – scale. I was used to giant, sprawling America where everything is epically vast. Not so in little England. I looked at the Tube map and worked out I needed to get on at Bond Street, which would then take me to Oxford Circus, not realizing that the entire journey, door-to-door from my apartment, takes ten minutes to walk. I gamely approached Marble Arch on my first day at Liberty of London, but there was another miscalculation. While the Tube is perfectly pleasant and spacious during weekends, rush hour is a different story. Crowds throng to the Tube like lines for Ellis Island in the 1800s. I remember waiting as several sardine-packed carriages went past. I ended up taking a running leap into an opportune crevice by the door, lodging myself between an armpit and the window, and vowing to take taxis in future. Nothing was worth this. Only later did I discover that walking would be quicker, and far nicer. Today, my walks to Liberty are my favourite morning ritual.

I prepared for my new role at Liberty by reading – a lot – about its history. Liberty's story was incredible and so inspiring. There's no store quite like it in the US, or anywhere on earth, for that matter. It had been founded in 1875 by Arthur Lasenby Liberty, a former merchant at London store Farmer and Rogers, with the aim of bringing trinkets, objects, rugs and gifts from around the world, from Asia to Africa, to surprise and delight Londoners, while also championing a new wave in British design and craftsmanship.

Arthur Liberty was a great visionary and took inspiration from all the international exhibitions in London which were celebrating the wonders of Britain's global empire. Meanwhile, the rise of the 'grand tour' – fuelled by commercial railways – had created an insatiable thirst for the exotic wares of foreign lands. Arthur wanted to create a store on Regent Street to bring all these inspiring pieces back to London – hence Liberty's emphasis on travel.

In 1885, Liberty bought a store space on Regent Street and soon Liberty was one of London's most popular emporiums, bedecked with rugs, sculptures and jewellery. Later, in the 1890s, it was a big supporter of the burgeoning British Arts and Crafts and art nouveau movements, collaborating with rising Arts and Crafts designers in London at the time, including William Morris and Gabriel Dante Rossetti. Liberty sold everything from Chinese and Japanese bronzes to enamels, jade and ceramics, embroideries and rugs from the Far East, antique European armour and coats of arms, and antique lace.

Early on, it also started printing fabrics. Shortly after opening the Liberty shop, Arthur Liberty printed the first Liberty silks. Imported from India, the Mysore silk was dyed and then hand-printed with wooden blocks in England. Liberty imported a number of oriental silks and had the growing selection of designs printed upon them in Scotland, Cumbria and Lancashire. In 1904, Liberty even bought his own print works, specializing in block-printed silks, near William Morris's production centre in Merton. Dubbed Merton Abbey Mills, it is set over the river Wandle, and can still be visited today (Morris's mill is now part of a craft and food market).

In 1924, such was Liberty's success that Arthur Liberty was able to extend his store. He bought the land on Great Marlborough Street and Kingly Street, and commissioned the great Tudor revival building we all know and love, using timbers from two old ships, HMS *Impregnable* and HMS *Hindustan*, designed by Edwin Thomas Hall (Tudor style was all the rage at this time). Hall designed it to feel like a Tudor home, with three light wells and several small rooms off each large space, as well as countless Tudor-style fireplaces. Though this contrasted markedly with the original stone Regent Street part of the store, the 'island' was rebuilt at a similar time as part of Regent Street's compulsory, uniform Beaux-Arts style. The two were connected by a Tudor-style bridge.

And there you have it. The landmark 1920s Tudor building is Grade II listed today. Its floors and beams almost create the feeling of being inside an old ship. Incidentally, I've always rather liked the connection to travel in the ship timber – it reinforces the fact that

Liberty discovers beautiful new pieces on its voyages.

Yet the place has evolved over the years. Today, Liberty of London sells homewares, beauty, fashion, jewellery, shoes, books, stationery and flowers. It's famous for its haberdashery – one of the last full-line haberdasheries in London, since people generally don't make or mend their own clothes 'full-time' any more. Today, a lot of the haberdashery is centred on arts and crafts, embroidery panels of Liberty prints for cushions and gifts, while also stocking Liberty fabric. The famous Liberty print archive, which includes forty thousand original designs, is also a sizeable part of its wholesale business. Liberty fabrics are sold the world over and are licensed to suitable partners in collaborations. We also have a Japanese subsidiary. New designs are introduced every season, while archived prints are intermittently re-released. Many Liberty prints are named after our staff.

People usually think only of the famous micro-floral motifs when they think of Liberty prints, but our fabrics have encompassed organic art nouveau patterns, decadent peacock feathers, darker, moodier and more romantic palettes, and at other times incredibly modern and painterly designs. More recently, Liberty has started playing with digital and photographic motifs, tapping into the new wave of London fashion designers, famed for their experimental *trompe-l'œil* and computer-manipulated designs. We have a large in-house team and frequently run print collaborations with fashion designers and British artists and illustrators such as Lauren Child, Eleanor Dorrien-Smith, Su Blackwell, Grayson Perry and Justine Smith.

Like any company of its age, Liberty of London has had its fair share of highs and lows over the century. It has expanded and contracted, added stores, lost stores. Today, its sole retail outlet is the Great Marlborough Street flagship, though it has an online shop, and a healthy fabric business.

For 125 years it was still operated by the family owners, the Stewart-Libertys, but in 2000, after years of battling between the family and the Liberty board, a controlling stake was sold to London property company Marylebone Warwick Balfour. Though Liberty's troubles didn't end there. In the early noughties, MWB itself faced financial distress, and in 2002 it announced that all its assets (including Liberty) would be sold in the next three years – thankfully, this didn't end up happening.

By 2005, MWB had managed to turn things around. They came up with a plan to sell several of the original – but less pivotal – Liberty-owned buildings surrounding the main store to generate some revenue and save the core business. It secured sufficient assets and was able to retain the main flagship. The buildings it sold included the front Beaux Arts part of the store on Regent Street, which is now occupied by COS and GAP among others – this frontage used to include Liberty's beauty department and featured grand cast-iron windows.

MWB also sold the neighbouring Lasenby House, on Kingly Street (which is now leased to Liberty and used as its staff offices). Walk around the streets surrounding Liberty and you can still see remnants of the original Liberty empire everywhere. The nearby pub, the Clachan, has a Liberty dining room. It really used to be a little Liberty neighbourhood. And, while it's a shame that the Regent Street frontage has gone, the move saved Liberty's future.

Geoffroy had been with Liberty since 2007 and had been tasked with updating the store. He had quickly bought in Yasmin Sewell in 2008, the respected consultant and former buyer for Browns Fashion, to assist on Liberty's revamp. When I joined, Yasmin – a willowy, dark-haired beauty with terrific style – had already begun work on cultivating more international brands. She'd also started to create what we would maximize at Liberty: a sense of edit. Yasmin and I would continue to work together on Liberty's fashion offer for the next two years, and we continue to work together even now.

When I arrived at 8.30 a.m. on my first day in December 2008, anxious as I was already late, it was somewhat of an anti-climax. Nobody was there. In New York it's not unusual for retail offices to be buzzing by 7.30 a.m., but at Liberty I couldn't even get into the buyer floor because it hadn't been opened yet. I sighed with relief as Judy, the eccentric, talkative receptionist, arrived at the door to let me in.

Anyone who's watched the Channel 4 *Liberty of London* documentary immediately adores Judy. She's an eccentric with a cockney accent, soft white-blonde hair, sparkly blue eyes, and an inexhaustible ability to chat. After a fifteen-minute conversation with Judy in which we exchanged life stories, personal aspirations and star signs, I wandered around until I found an office with a blank desk and some bits of equipment with my name on. I then sat, in silence, wondering what to do.

It was only after 9.30 a.m. that the first buyers started to dribble in. Then I realized my second error. Grown in the Bergdorf Goodman suits-and-boots mould, I had arrived at Liberty in suit and tie, complete with pocket square, only to see a series of sweaters, unbuttoned shirts and denim walk past. Oh no! For the first time in my career I felt the panicked need to dress down, not up. More adjustments.

With big plans for Liberty's 'Renaissance' in 2009, I had to hit the ground running. To begin with, it was the run-up to Christmas and the floors were packed with shoppers. A big relaunch was planned for early in the New Year but in the meantime I knew I needed to implement some changes quickly. I started working my way through the list of tasks I'd detailed in that first walk through back in 2007, starting with maximizing Liberty's floor space.

Unlike the sprawling halls of Harrods or Selfridges, Liberty of London has a serious space issue. In 2008, Liberty had just 70,000 square feet of selling space, while Selfridges had 540,000 square feet. Harrods has over 1,000,000 square feet in selling space and occupies five acres! Where some stores can simply renovate or extend, Liberty had limited funds, limited space, and was also Grade II listed, which in practice means touch one of those beams and you'll be hanged, or shot, or both, within minutes.

I had no illusions of doubling the size of Liberty with a magical six-floor subterranean basement – though I'd love to see the planners' faces at that application! But in retail, space is money, so every inch needed to be maximized for selling. I set about streamlining every tiny piece of wasted space in the building and turning it over to retail, which meant getting rid of that ground-floor stationery stockroom. Liberty's buyer offices were then on the fourth floor of the main store, which I also promptly adjusted. We moved – as soon as I could arrange it – to separate offices, and eventually to Lasenby House.

Having freed up space on the fourth floor for more retail, I also did an audit of vacant or disused spaces that we'd later renovate and convert to retail. I discovered, with a sense of excitement but also abject horror, empty decrepit rooms on every single floor above ground in the corner of the store that overlooks Carnaby Street – prime retail estate. These were later converted into a personal shopping suite, Margaret Dabbs Sole Spa, and Josh Wood Atelier Hair Lab. By the time we were finished, Liberty's retail space had increased to 80,000 square feet – though I'm still trying to eke out extra inches. The grandest of my (as yet unrealized) endeavours has been to turn all of Little Marlborough Street, the small alley at the back of Liberty, into a shopping street, with windows all along the ground-floor side and a new extra entrance with awnings over the top.

Part of Geoffroy's grand plan for Liberty was to give it a credible voice in fashion, which meant extending the one single floor of women's ready-to-wear into two. This was one of my first major challenges. Liberty was known for gifts, for homewares, for textiles, but fashion? Not so much – at least not at that time. Yasmin had begun bringing in brands including Donna Karan and Calvin Klein but still, we needed to fill two floors, while also conducting a cull on the vast number of unnecessary brands Liberty was selling. We ended up cutting some four hundred in order to streamline the offer.

There were bigger challenges afoot at Liberty of London, too. It still needed the dust blowing off it in a major way. This meant identifying, and refining, exactly what Liberty stood for, or needed to stand for in its new iteration.

Angela Ahrendts had warned me about the challenges and joys of coming to work on a heritage brand – and that's essentially what Liberty is. People have strong feelings about national treasures and Liberty, as they do Burberry. It is steeped in British culture, and the British have deeply rooted perceptions of what it should be. I needed to find a way to update this heritage, to make it relevant and profitable without seeming like the evil American import destroying a London gem.

This came down to branding. In the ecosystem of brands, there are of course 'brand' brands, but department stores are also brands, and Liberty is its own brand. People can shop anywhere, but when it comes to big old stores like Liberty, they shop there because they like what it stands for. But who were we now? What was Liberty? For me, this had been lost. We needed it to have a point of view again, keeping the story but removing its cobwebs.

Liberty will never be the size of its London department store neighbours, but to try and emulate them is to miss the point. People come to Liberty, and have always come to Liberty, due to its handpicked treasures and special edit. We are not a department store, we cannot physically offer the full range of everything as the vast halls of concessions in Selfridges do, so our best hope of succeeding was to play to this as an advantage and think more like a concept store. A big concept store, but a concept store nonetheless. This would become our strategy.

Concept stores, to the uninitiated, were born in the nineties, with leading examples being Carla Sozzani's 10 Corso Como in Milan and, later, Colette in Paris. The idea with concept stores is just that, an idea. They are boutiques selling a range of homewares, books, clothing, objets d'art, music and jewellery, edited with a single point of view – often the owner's – into which people can buy. They are highly curated, and often occupy smaller spaces. Their products, from books to teapots, are presented together, rather than by separate 'departments'. The effect is almost like a magazine, and the stocks are often switched around regularly on this basis, to make them feel like they're constantly evolving, changing and always surprising.

It sounds ludicrous today but when these kinds of stores first emerged, they were seen as revolutionary – flowers next to books and shoes? Teapots next to beauty? But this notion has since become a huge influence on retail and the way retail environments are designed. Just think about Urban Outfitters today, for example, or Anthropologie, or even And Other Stories, the fashion and beauty chain owned by H&M. All of these are curated; they mix different products in their merchandising, and their interiors are forever subject to rearrangement. They are also intentionally made to feel local, artisan, and almost independent. This all came from concept stores. It was the kind of fresh approach I thought would work perfectly for Liberty. In many ways, I like to think Liberty in the 1800s was the original 'concept store': an emporium of wonders curated by Arthur.

So what was Liberty's concept now? How could we bring that vision of Arthur Liberty into the twenty-first century? I decided on a framework for Liberty's brand, something that incorporated its past, its heritage, and what it should be today, and used that as a construct, or filter, through which to make all decisions about the store. I scribbled on a pad of paper within days of starting at Liberty, from my Marylebone studio, 'Liberty of London is: craftsmanship but with a relaxed attitude; quirk; Britishness; luxury; unique; special and global.' Sound about right? From there, it became simple.

By establishing this voice, it provided a guide – one that we would use to correct Liberty's product and brand offer, which had sprawled to include everything from hosiery to racing hats. We needed to adjust this, ensuring that each floor felt like it had been bought and edited all with the same eye.

We culled those four hundred brands from its offer, but in doing so we also made way for some exciting new ones. London-based Eskandar, designed by Eskandar Nabavi, was an easy addition, and perfect for Liberty's loyal customers. This lifestyle brand, which focuses on oversize linen separates and tunics with clean, modern lines, is hugely successful in New York and was perfect for Liberty's design-savvy clientele. Everyone looks great in this brand and it has since proven a hit with our customers.

By the time I'd finished, we had Alexander Wang, Rag & Bone, Victoria Beckham, Vince, J. Brand, Carven, McQ, Mother of Pearl, Opening Ceremony, Kenzo and Phillip Lim among many others, slotting nicely into a chicly edited contemporary brand and casual floor; and the more formal floor with international designers such as Dries Van Noten, The Row and Marni.

One of the obvious things lacking in our fashion offer, and absent from the 'British' part of the Liberty brand framework, funnily enough, was British design. It seemed insane that, as a British institution, Liberty of London did not stock Stella McCartney – so I bought her in right away. We also bought in Roland Mouret, whose female-friendly, figure-flattering designs were so right for the Liberty woman. The women who come to Liberty want something special, but something that makes them *feel* special, and his dresses (expertly cut – I defy anyone to look bad in them) have been a consistent hit ever since we introduced them.

Yasmin had already been working with the British Fashion Council to support our roster of young British talent and with their NEWGEN committee (industry mentors), while bringing in young British designers. Liberty now sells a host of British labels, including Roksanda, Christopher Kane, Peter Pilotto, Jonathan Saunders and many more. Later, we also launched a collaborative collection with Erdem. We were the first retailer to stock rising talent Michael van der Ham – his dressmaker-inspired, collage approach to design again, I felt, sat perfectly with Liberty's pillars.

I'm proud to say that in my time since joining Liberty I've truly got to know and love the British fashion community. The British Fashion Council under its chief executive Caroline Rush has transformed London Fashion Week, bringing in tons of business support – just what was needed – internationalizing it, and winning valuable press exposure. I have come to work regularly with British talents such as *Love* magazine editor Katie Grand and the designers Katie Hillier, Luella Bartley, Victoria Beckham and Stella McCartney. More recently, I've introduced a Liberty-sponsored scholarship at the London College of Fashion to continue Liberty's legacy of supporting new British design talent.

The other thing, which I have continued to ramp up since joining Liberty, is the store's sense of humour. Yes, Liberty is a heritage brand. Yes, it stands for craftsmanship, luxury and beautiful design but, being British, it can also laugh at itself. From amusing antique curiosities to quirky prints (now including those designed by the cross-dressing artist Grayson Perry) and its window displays, we try to keep a sense of wit in everything.

This kind of humour can be very helpful when working on a brand. It provides you with a degree of elasticity and freedom to take risks, doing things beyond the boundaries of that which would traditionally be deemed luxury. Just ask Anya Hindmarch; it's enabled her to sell her beautiful £800 leather handbags in glittery toy boxes, or attach lollipops to fashion show invites without anyone batting an eyelid. Or think Kenzo, which has played with the idea of ironic logos in its Kenzo-emblazoned sweaters and caps in recent years, becoming a retail phenomenon. Executed well, it can be really charming and inclusive, and still feel luxurious too.

Playfulness also injects a sense of youth into a brand. I like to think we've recently emphasized more of this at Liberty. For the royal nuptials between Prince William and Kate Middleton, rather than be lofty, we played on the idea of true tourist kitsch, printing our own playful mugs and tea towels with their images on. For the Queen's Diamond Jubilee, we created royal pincushions. We've had gospel choirs and drag queens appear at events. It's had a lot to do with bringing energy back to the place.

The less glamorous side of streamlining a store like Liberty and directing it to profitability is to look beyond the parties and marketing, to its numbers. Alongside becoming more visible, we needed to make the business more efficient, and that meant having some tough conversations.

One of the key things we immediately started out trying to change was our relationship with vendors. Liberty had lost a bit of its confidence in 2008, and that showed in our dealings with suppliers, who often behaved as if they were doing us a favour by selling to us.

Retail in my view should be about collaboration, a partnership between the vendor and the store. A vendor isn't doing you a favour by selling to you, and should contribute equally to making sure the merchandise sells, whether it's through assisting in launches, with press, or in promotions. You both want, and need, a product line to sell. It's why brands often share the cost with the retailer for promotional store magazines and shoots. Because they know it's good business.

I'd been used to this in New York at Bergdorf Goodman, so was shocked to find that Liberty received none of this help in London, despite the store being very powerful in terms of influence. We were given stock, and that was that. A few of our existing brands got a tough wake-up call when I arrived and told them 'this is not going to work for us any more'. We lost a few in the process, including one very global luxury brand, but it was worth it. Sometimes you have to respect yourself.

Liberty of London when I joined had two main core customer bases, which were strong, but needed to evolve if we were to grow. We had a loyal, fifty-plus, older customer locked in. This group remain hugely important to Liberty and we are grateful to have them all, but if you're thinking about the future of your business, the reality is that they are also shrinking, retiring, or whichever more elegant way you wish to term it. This customer needs to be maintained, has money to spend, time to browse, and an increasingly youthful outlook, but they will only shop less in the next twenty years. We needed to keep them happy, while also diversifying to attract a younger audience.

Then we have the locals and tourists. These are constants at Liberty but they, too, keep you on your toes. You have to have the right product offer, which means British trinkets and Liberty print wares for the tourists and exciting gifts for the locals – I've often seen panicked women scooping armfuls of Diptyque for office leaving presents.

Both of our original consumer bases are important and valuable, but what we didn't have in 2008 was the growing younger demographic – those pesky twenty-somethings. They may have shopped in Liberty with their mothers as children, but at this point they weren't shopping in Liberty for beauty or fashion. These were young professional shoppers splurging on handbags, luxury T-shirts, Space NK makeup and designer shoes. Liberty just didn't have them.

We wanted to get young shoppers through our doors without alienating our loyal older, tourist and local customers. This has not been straightforward. The truth is that age, background and demographic are increasingly unquantifiable in terms of taste. People shop outside their age, and very confidently, so that it becomes less about pigeonholing with product to a specific group and more about focusing on having the best available products in any category to shop in-store.

Preconceived notions of what some customers want are in a state of total flux right now. As such – I believe – they must be reviewed to be successful. Eskandar definitely has a loyal older consumer base at Liberty but, increasingly, fifty-something consumers, particularly women still working in high-powered jobs, want contemporary high fashion, not tunics, stilettos or sandals. I'll tour the floors of Liberty and see as many fifty-plus women trying on Peter Pilotto and Dries Van Noten as twenty-somethings (God knows they're more likely to be able to afford it). All the rules have disappeared.

Haberdashery – previously synonymous with old ladies – is often packed with twenty-somethings in search of knitting needles or Liberty micro-floral fabrics. It's the same with gender. Visit the beauty department on a given day, and chances are there will be nearly as many men looking at premium skincare as women. Murdock, our men's grooming salon in the basement, is frequently fully booked by grooming-addicted men, connoisseurs of beard upkeep. You have to adapt and ensure you have something for everybody, and the way to do this is simply to make sure your product is amazing.

This is a shift, which I only saw increasing when I joined Liberty in 2008 and, sure enough, it becomes more apparent with every passing year. Consumers have access to limitless information from the internet, blogs and magazines, and don't buy into dictates in the same way they did before. They want to make their own choices and have complete confidence in doing so. They're also less influenced by trend. It's started to work outwards from personal style as opposed to buying into a prescribed movement.

If I learned anything from my time at Henri Bendel about re-energizing a store, it's that getting people talking is a major part of it. If you don't have giant budgets and a PR agency this also means being creative. The nice thing about Liberty of London is that the fashion press in the UK have a big affection for us, so as we started introducing new initiatives, they were well received. (No more snarky comments about 'buzz'. Buzz was good. And buzz was exactly what we needed in 2009 if our 'Renaissance' was to work.)

Following on from Henri Bendel's Open Call events, I started staging similar Open Design Days at Liberty, inviting fashion, and furniture, silver and ceramic designers to come in and show their wares. For the first one, we created a panel, which included myself, Yasmin Sewell, and *Vogue* fashion journalist Sarah Mower. We had an overwhelming response and it got picked up right away in the fashion press.

Early on in my time at Liberty, we also collaborated with Kate Moss on her collection for Topshop, allowing her to use hand-picked archive prints for her pieces that summer. I must admit to a secret moment of pride when Kate Moss was quoted saying how much of a long-term fan she was of Liberty prints. At the same time, sensing a 'Liberty print moment', we took advantage by staging an exhibition of our prints in-store, entitled *Prints Charming*, and showcasing archive designs and special new prints created by collaborators such as artist Grayson Perry, a fan of, and regular customer at, Liberty. Perry came to the opening of the event in full costume, to celebrate his prints – a surreal and cartoonish mixture of teddy bears and darker motifs, such as tombstones and eerie faces.

By August 2009 there were already signs that this approach was working. We weren't quite in profit, but our losses were shrinking and our sales were up (a shrinking loss! I'll take that). After nine months in London, having taken this enormous life gamble, it was incredibly encouraging.

I'd also started to settle into London life. It's the nuances you pick up when you live somewhere. Americans will always have an umbrella on them, for example. And yet the Brits, in a country where it rains constantly, appear not to. Baffling. They also have a fear of aspartame akin to fear of the devil. This is a US thing, and also partly my age – we Baby Boomers love sweeteners. I will happily pour into my coffee Splenda sachets galore, and woe betide any restaurant that doesn't serve Diet Coke. I have even installed a vending machine in Liberty's buying offices.

I've come, eventually, to accept the UK's strict planning restrictions. Liberty's store is Grade II listed, which means you cannot even paint a wall without checking in. Forget knocking down a pillar, or moving it. The store was designed to emulate a domestic Tudor residence, which is romantic in theory but means it is tough to merchandise and sell effectively (which is kind of the point, as a store). The building has narrow corridors, dark rooms, endless nooks and big spaces which the light from the skylight can't quite reach. But, at the same time, there are amazing period details, including countless fireplaces – every time we renovate we seem to discover a new one. The staircase also features a hand-carved memorial in the panelling to the soldiers from Liberty who participated in the First World War.

We ended up using period detail as a decorative construct when we came to transform the homewares department on the fourth floor. Returning to Liberty's Arts and Crafts heritage, we wanted to create a department selling original Arts and Crafts furniture. Arthur Liberty was integral to supporting the Arts and Crafts Movement so I thought it fitting to sell the antiques in their native setting. We worked with expert dealers who scoured the markets to find originals; they returned with some incredible one-off pieces. The department was nothing short of magical. It's a real Arts and Crafts 'home', with chairs and desks carefully arranged around the fireplaces like living rooms.

I have adapted to Liberty's dress style since joining, though this took some psychological renegotiating. Dressing casually aged twenty-five is one thing (skinny jeans, thrift-store shirts) but at fifty it's a delicate art. You want to look respectable and authoritative, yet simultaneously relaxed and youthful – the right side of youthful, not grandpa in a tracksuit! I've since settled into a uniform of clean-cut, crisp white shirts (and yes, I still have them dry-cleaned), jeans, layering over jackets or knitwear in winter, and a great scarf. It's no accident that Liberty's menswear department has become a hub for the man-scarf, or 'marf', as *Grazia* magazine journalists would dub it. That's another thing I've come to love about London. *Grazia*-isms . . .

***

After a year of settling in I also started to explore the UK, though again had to adjust to the scale of things. I visited Brighton, packing a book, an apple, and some lunch for the journey, thinking it would take the whole day to get there. The coastline seemed eons away from London on the map. I was there in just over fifty minutes, and back in time for cocktail hour.

One of my most memorable visits was to Prospect Cottage, the home of film director and artist Derek Jarman, in Dungeness on the barren coast of Kent. I am fascinated by Derek Jarman – his film *Blue* really struck a chord with me. The film was released in 1993, four months before his death from AIDS-related complications. Jarman had gone partially blind, just like my best friend, Dean, in New York. The film is a single shot of blue that fills the screen, as actors narrate his life and vision, or recite poetry. It's utterly compelling. In the eighties, Jarman had bought this old tar-painted fisherman's cottage in Dungeness, Kent. In the 1990s, just before he died, he wrote a book, *Garden*, in which he tells of creating the garden there in the shadow of the nearby Dungeness nuclear power station.

Anyone who's been to this area will know its bleak beauty. It's like a flat desert of pebbles (it's actually classified as Britain's only desert), with the nuclear plant in the background. In Jarman's book, he talks of working on Prospect Cottage in the shingles, creating a vegetable patch, planting flowers and creating sculptures. It's the most incredible place; there are no boundaries to the garden, it just kind of sprawls. Everywhere, there are small sculptural details made from reclaimed wood or found objects, that you only pick up on closer look, and which have been arranged in a certain way. You feel him all around you. On the side of the cottage is a poem in 3-D text, also in black, so you have to concentrate to read it – 'The Sun Rising', by John Donne.

The house's deep, jet-black wooden cladding contrasts brilliantly with lemon-yellow window frames. Having my own house in Montauk, which I only visit in winter when it's totally empty, I warmed to the feeling of isolation there. I could see why he loved it so much.

I also started to make friends in London, though I did escape back to the US frequently for buying trips, to check in on my house in Montauk, or visit my parents. At this stage, Mum and Dad had moved to Florida, the retirement capital of North America, to live the good life in the sunshine. Intermittently, I'd fly back to see them and stay for a few days.

From my Henri Bendel days onwards, I'd re-embraced my parents, in part because my mother's health was deteriorating and I wanted to see her more regularly, but also because I had become a success. My frequent returns home in varying states of disrepair in my early twenties had been marked by sheepishness on my part – I was coming home because I needed them and had nowhere else to go. I'd drive up to the house and always feel a bit embarrassed.

When I started doing well, it changed our whole dynamic. One of the biggest turning points on this front was when my father said to me at Henri Bendel: 'I don't know where you got the brains from, Ed.' He says that to me every time we speak on the phone and it still makes me emotional. He is very proud of me.

In recent years I've become much closer to my father. My mother, who died in early 2014, suffered from Alzheimer's disease. In her later years she no longer recognized me, so when I returned it was mainly my father to whom I spoke. Perhaps due to his late stage in life, Dad has only become funnier. He always had a terrific sense of humour but now he's retired, he's embraced morbid 'ticking clock' humour. Everything is about, 'Not long now, Ed. If this cake doesn't kill me, nothing will.' It's dark, but we do laugh.

And though my mother's last years were probably a blur to her, she and I also spent good times together in Florida. I would take her for drives after she got sick, windows rolled down, warm Florida breeze running through her hair as she gazed out at the beach, or the highway. We'd have strange moments of closeness. She'd spontaneously put her hand on top of mine as if she knew who I was again. I know, of course, that she probably didn't, but I like to think, at least on an instinctive level, that she did.

Six months in at Liberty, and the tide was turning. That early sales leap preceded a series of coups in 2009, both in terms of sales and recognition.

We launched a Hermès collaboration and pop-up shop for scarves and ties. Hermès is very discriminating about its collaborators. In other words, it doesn't collaborate! But because of Liberty's long heritage in prints, it was a perfect fit. In a retail coup, the brand created a limited-edition capsule collection for us and we staged a Hermès pop-up in-store. Naturally, we went to town with this, hosting scarf-tying workshops and introducing 'scarf stylists' to the department. It was picked up everywhere.

We continued to build buzz with great, timely collaborations. In 2009, fashion blogging and fashion-photo blogging had become a sensation, breeding a new type of coverage and homegrown superstar. In the front row, alongside Anna Wintour and Suzy

Menkes, suddenly bloggers like Bryanboy, Susie Bubble and Tommy Ton were seated to review the clothes (much to the chagrin of established fashion press). Meanwhile, outside every fashion show were street-style bloggers.

Of all of them, Scott Schuman, 'The Sartorialist', was a trailblazer and most well known. Having started his blog in 2005 by snapping stylish people in their clothes, he'd risen to the status of fashion darling by 2009, shooting for brands like Burberry. Liberty played host to the launch of his debut book *The Sartorialist*, a collection of his favourite pictures. The signing was packed with fans. Yasmin, Jefferson Hack and Tim Blanks also attended. More flashbulbs for us.

Liberty's momentum continued through until Christmas that year. The store had started to get a real energy to it. The year was capped by a special Luella Bartley-themed Christmas shopping event, complete with kitsch ornaments, grotto, and exclusive Luella gifts. We ramped up the campness for the party, too, with candy canes, cider, carol singers, and Father Christmas. Katie Hillier, Jake Chapman, David Sims, Serena Rees and Stevie Nicks came along.

I almost didn't notice, as I cheered with the rest of them for the tubby Santa Claus arrival, that I'd been there for a year. A whole year? I'd made it. Somehow. It's funny; I could tell I'd finally settled here when I sat on my sofa one evening regarding my apartment. In the early months, my renter-chic beige furnishings dominated the space, but by December I'd started cluttering it up with knick-knacks. (The inescapable knick-knacks. My childhood bedroom all over again.)

Piles of coffee-table books sat on benches, not to mention those overpriced scented candles. Meanwhile, I'd bought paintings and prints to line the walls. I'd even bought a British bulldog ornament and Union Jack cushion. More importantly, the staff at Liberty had started to like me. Liberty, as anyone who has seen the Channel 4 documentary will know, plays host to a colourful cast of characters – some long in the tooth, some crazy, all funny, and all kind. They'd accepted me as the incumbent American. If only I knew what 2010 would bring – a promotion, several more years at Liberty, and much more.

CHAPTER 7

THE TOP JOB AT LIBERTY: MANAGING DIRECTOR, TV AND BEYOND

Cogs at Liberty had started turning in the right direction at the start of 2010, at least to the outside world. We were in the press. We had great collections. The store had been streamlined. Our sales increases were being enthusiastically reported in the press (gliding over the disconnection between sales increases and actual profit). We were back.

Behind closed doors, however, there were difficulties at Liberty. I didn't admit it to myself at the time, but I was finding working under Geoffroy frustrating. I was living and breathing the store day in, day out, and that familiarity meant I was seeing more and more changes that needed making to the business. But at that stage I did not have the authority to make them. As buying director, I was in charge of the day-to-day minutiae at Liberty, but I had no say in the bigger, wider strategy of the store. Although Geoffroy was very accomplished, part of me disagreed with some of the moves he was making.

While the store itself had been doing much better, big areas of the business were also struggling. From 2004, Liberty's owners had tried to set up a separate Liberty of London luxury brand, headed up by Tamara Salman as creative director (Tamara had previously worked in-house at Prada and Romeo Gigli). By the time I joined Liberty, the brand had expanded to include bags, swimwear, leather goods, scarves and neckties, and had a self-contained team of almost fifty people in a separate office. Salman, in creating this modern Liberty of London 'brand', had moved away from the traditional Liberty micro-florals and embraced the company's rich archive art nouveau prints, which had moodier palettes, and often peacock feather motifs. She also created sumptuous handbags and leather accessories as the key 'investment' pieces, hoping to tap into the luxury accessories boom at the time.

The company had initially been bullish with Liberty of London, and had even launched a lavish Sloane Square flagship for the Liberty brand, designed by architects Pierre Beucler and Jean-Christophe Poggioli with opulent furnishings and Liberty's iconic crest on the front doors. There were also signs of success early on – the brand was stocked in Jeffrey in New York and 10 Corso Como in Milan. But something about it didn't resonate with consumers, at least not in a way that justified its overheads. In February 2010, Salman left the brand and soon after, the Liberty of London Sloane Street store was shut – in part because Moncler made an opportune offer to take over the lease. The brand was soon phased out.

It was sad, not only for the talented team involved but also because the brand was nicely executed. It just goes to prove that it's not as easy as it looks to enter the luxury market.

We were able to showcase the Liberty brand in other ways in 2010 though, using the huge resource that is its print archives.

Liberty prints are perfect for collaborations. They are a huge asset to the company and can be applied to any number of products and be instantly recognizable as 'Liberty'.

Around February 2010 we collaborated with US retail giant Target on a capsule collection featuring our signature florals, which is possibly – even now – one of our highest-profile collections to date.

Before Target I'd been reticent about doing a collaboration with retailers of this size, simply because in previous meetings with similar-sized behemoths, the quality of the finished pieces was questionable. And by questionable, I mean disgraceful. Liberty was about quality, even if it was on the high street, and we had to protect that. No one had passed muster.

But then Target appeared and won me over. The pieces looked amazing. They were all beautifully produced with attention to detail and brilliant depth of colour, which was faithful to the original Liberty print designs. More importantly, Target seemed to really get the idea of bringing Liberty print to the masses in a fresh way. It was special, premium, not part of the mainline Target offer, and their whole approach was tailored to this.

We went ahead and it was a huge success. Target opened a special Liberty-themed pop-up shop in Bryant Park, New York. They created a small garden space with moving digital projections of Liberty prints everywhere on the walls. Meanwhile, our signature florals were splashed onto candles, bedding, gardening tools and stationery. They also launched it with a big TV and print campaign. The collaboration made Liberty visible on the US stage.

We took a multi-faceted approach with collaborations. Around the same time as Target we also teamed with iconic Milanese concept store, 10 Corso Como, for a capsule collection.

We launched it with a cocktail during London Fashion Week and the store founder, Carla Sozzani, and Anna Wintour, swung by. We also continued the 'concept store' connection by collaborating with famed Paris concept store Merci soon after. In the same month, all of Merci, which borders the Marais neighbourhood in Paris, was taken over with Liberty print products, from mugs to mini briefcases to aprons.

First the US, then Paris. The Liberty word was spreading.

It was around 2010 that reports first surfaced about a possible sale of Liberty from its current owners MWB Group Holdings. The sale of the building, to begin with, was intended to raise extra funds for Liberty. The freehold would be sold by MWB to another owner, and leased back to Liberty to release money for investing in the store. To me, while unsettling, the move was encouraging. We'd started making improvements at Liberty but needed a major cash injection to lead the regeneration of the store, especially for the bigger ideas I'd been cooking up in my head.

Then, in May, the bigger news broke. Liberty was sold after a bidding war to former City bankers BlueGem Capital Partners, a private equity group, for £32 million.

There was an element of uncertainty when the sale was confirmed. There always is in buyouts, as new owners have the option of sweeping out senior management or of keeping the existing team. For me, it marked a turning point in my commitment to Liberty and the UK. It could have been an easy break back to the US; I had done a decent amount of time as buying director and achieved a lot while there, but I wasn't ready to return. I knew Liberty could be so much more.

Apart from anything else, I was keen to stay because I'd finally be getting a US friend in town. It had just been announced that Scott would take up his new role at Kurt Geiger, transplanting him to London. I'd already started scoping out places for him in Bermondsey, near the Kurt Geiger offices, but within days of his arrival he called me: 'Ed, I've got a place. Don't worry. It's in this neighbourhood called . . . Marylebone? Do you know it?' I had to laugh.

I'd become somewhat of a local in Marylebone by this point, swimming in the nearby pool every Saturday, my favourite thing, and training in the park three times a week. (Necessary when you're fifty: as anyone this age will know, it becomes less about self-improvement and more about working harder and harder to look exactly the same.)

Though on one occasion I probably got to know my neighbours a little too well. Throughout my life, I have had issues with sleepwalking, especially if I have taken a Valium before bed. I also sleep in Y-fronts. It was the perfect storm one evening during this time: a glass of red, a Valium, and exhaustion from a flight. I went to bed and without realizing, managed to get up in the night, walk out of my apartment and out of the front door. It was only the contact of my feet on the freezing, damp front step of my apartment block that jolted me awake. I managed to get back inside the building, but was locked out of my apartment in a freezing cold lobby. Still foggy from the wine, I decided the only option was to sleep by my front door, grabbing a children's blanket from a stroller in the corridor to keep me warm, and curl up on the doormat. This worked for about thirty minutes, but was obviously not a long-term solution. Then a drunken neighbour came in, but rather than offer me help, he simply handed me some pyjama bottoms and slammed the door. He didn't even seem shocked, which was odd to me in the following days when I relived the entire ridiculous scenario. Eventually, emboldened and desperate, I decided to make a break for it. Scott's house was two blocks away and if I went really fast – even though I was barefoot and only wearing pyjama bottoms – it would be better than spending the night in the hall. Scott let me in, after my knocking heavily on his door for what seemed like hours. It was 5 a.m. by then. Amid all this drama, we had a quick glass of wine before grabbing an hour or two of sleep. Somehow it felt just about right after all that trauma; the birds tweeting with the sunrise, and a glass of Pinot Noir.

The games weren't over yet, though. I didn't have any clothes and my spare key was at work. Scott is shorter and broader than me, and I had to borrow a suit of his to go into work the next day. I looked like a tramp. It was the one security guard I didn't know and I showed up with trousers gaping around my ankles, rambling on about my key. 'No really! I work here!' Suffice to say, I now wear full pyjamas to bed.

***

BlueGem was headed up by the former director of Merrill Lynch, Marco Capello, a dark-haired Italian gentleman and a formidable business operator. I remember the day he and the other BlueGem executives first came into Liberty for a boardroom meeting to discuss their new acquisition. Water was poured, the tablecloths were starched, and in they marched.

BlueGem were a hugely successful company. Their portfolio outside of this included a Harley Street clinic and an energy company. Marco took to the floor, expressing his enthusiasm for

Liberty and its future, as new investors often do, before starting to scribble on the large flip-pad his plans for changes to Liberty.

Something inside me flipped at this point. Marco is without question a trailblazing businessman. At just thirty-four, he was made head of investment banking for Merrill Lynch in Italy. From 2002 to 2006 he was a managing director of Merrill Lynch Global Private Equity, handling investments worth €650 million. This was my opportunity to show him my vision for Liberty. I leapt up, my palms sweating, and grabbed the pen from him before I could think about it too much.

'Here's what you should do,' I said, scribbling on the flat plans. 'I'd double beauty. I'd move this here. I'd move this here.' I gathered so much momentum sketching that I didn't stop to think about if it seemed brash. It was only when I handed back the pen, exhaling slightly, that I realized this could have gone down very badly indeed. But the show of strength was perfectly timed, it turns out. It proved I knew what I was talking about and that gave Marco confidence in me. He must have felt that way anyway, because shortly after Geoffroy stepped down I was promoted to managing director of the store. Marco, meanwhile, became executive chairman.

Here I was again. A whole store to play with, and only the slightest hint of pressure. My new role, in addition to buying director, included overseeing everything from the buy, to press, marketing and the Liberty of London brand. But I couldn't wait. I had, at this point, totally fallen for Liberty, London, and the UK – hook, line and sinker. I'd also become excited at the prospect of seeing Liberty fly again.

To BlueGem's credit they listened to me, which sounds obvious, but so often when private equity companies buy new ventures they think they need to get external help to 'save' them, or turn them around. The staff at Liberty were totally capable. We knew what to do. Liberty was not broken, it just needed some love. We were left, after Geoffroy departed, a lean team of four heading up Liberty plc.

People often think that I am in charge of everything at Liberty plc, perhaps because I am the most visible senior member of staff, but in addition to Marco, three people currently run this company, one for each of its key revenue streams. I head up buying for the store (the brand, the stuff, the running, the marketing). There is Sarah Halsall, directing operations, overseeing our online and wholesale business. Debra Wood is our chief financial officer. We work together as a well-oiled team.

Marco was very open to our input. On a retail standpoint when BlueGem took over, he also brought in a very businesslike approach to the numbers. BlueGem invested a massive amount of money in new updates, renovations and additions to Liberty, and each had to be approached with a solid business case and projected return on investment. But the point is, they were open to it. Rational generosity – it was music to my ears. They have since devoted, and continue to devote, a lot of money to maintaining the Tudor building, because it's good for business.

Sarah Halsall and I in particular have come to be great friends since working together at Liberty – the dynamic duo of ringing tills, both physical and digital. She's the type that will not suffer fools gladly, that's for sure, but will also laugh. She is extremely authentic, for want of a less irritating word. You won't get fluff from her. I'm also really inspired by what she's done at Liberty. I still direct the 'stuff', but thanks to her we're not limited to the four corners of this Tudor building any more. Globally, anyone can shop from Liberty online and receive perfectly wrapped purple packages to their door. Our e-commerce business has quadrupled under her stewardship.

Marco and I have also worked well together. The best thing is his passion for Liberty. He truly believes in it and wants it to succeed. He's shrewd, extremely sharp and his mind works faster than anyone else's I know – you get ten good minutes to put points to him, then he's onto the next thing. Like Sarah, he doesn't work with fluff or over-elaboration. But he's also very human and funny. Perhaps it's his Italian heritage – he seems to have a life story to illustrate any point he is making. I have come to be really fond of these anecdotes. The other key thing with Marco is that he respects you enough to let you get on with things.

I've also come to rationalize my approach to Liberty since joining. I am not a creative person, but neither am I all about numbers. I have a business background but an appreciation for creativity, and I actually think this is perfectly suited to Liberty. If you go too much towards the right brain (the creative side), you end up where we were before, making losses. But, if you go too left brain (the pragmatic side), you lose the Liberty magic. Somehow, I have honed myself to be a middle-way director. By the same token, I am not – as my TV persona would have it – a tyrant manager. But nor am I a teddy bear. I am nice, but when I need to talk business I do.

The buyout brought a great energy to Liberty. Marco was interviewed extensively in the press and outlined our big plans. We'd continue our Open Call event for new designers. We'd be extending the fine jewellery department (fashion fine jewellery was exploding at this time). We'd be adding more fashion brands to Liberty, including Phillip Lim and Alexander Wang, while building up denim and contemporary ready-to-wear. Soon after we would also overhaul our homewares edit.

The menswear department from this point on also started to take on its own identity. Stephen Ayres, then the menswear buyer (he is now head of all fashion buying), established the basement men's floor as a hub for cool men's casual brands, new accessories, and great street wear – cutting all the other junk to make it a slick menswear destination.

Stephen, a slim young man with brown hair and brown eyes, has a boyishly innocent smile, which fools many. He is one of our top buyers and has moved from transforming menswear to working on Liberty's entire fashion offer.

Liberty's menswear department is his crowning glory, though. Not a Saturday passes when walking through the men's floor that you cannot spot editors and stylists from all the men's fashion magazines perusing the rails, or having a beer and a haircut in Murdock's barber. It's become a total hangout, where fashion-conscious boys – be they gay, straight, stylist, banker, executive or musician – will come to shop side by side.

Part of Liberty's rebirth was about getting new things into the store, and for that I returned to my old Open Call format, championed previously at Henri Bendel.

To this day, Open Call is one of my favourite achievements at Liberty. It's become pivotal in discovering new, incredible talent. I remember at the first one, a ceramic and wood homewares designer, Thomas Hopkins-Gibson, travelled all the way down from northern Scotland to show us his pieces. Tom, an unassuming Scot, is unfailingly modest about his work, but when he reached into his case to show us his pieces, we were astounded. They were beautiful, so much so that I ventured up to Scotland to see him work in situ.

Tom lives and works in a small house on a small sliver of beach, surrounded by rugged cliffs either side and rolling hills behind. Each day he walks across to the beach opposite and picks out pieces of washed up wood he likes the look of, which he then carves into exquisite wooden bowls. He also produces hand-made ceramics, using the grain of local natural wood to create a patterned textured effect on the outside. We fell in love with him and his story, and have stocked his collection ever since.

We also discovered Christopher Raeburn, a young London-based menswear designer. Christopher is a tall, blond and confident man, and we were impressed by his slick designs that reclaim and reuse materials, transforming them into slick urban garments. We also found Richard Weston, a scarf designer from Wales. Richard is a teacher and architect by trade, and came to us with beautiful silk prints, which he made using a special technique, shining light through splices of gemstones to generate beautiful motifs, which he then transferred onto fabric. He showed up with great reams of silk covered in these beautiful gemstone designs, and we worked with him to create a scarf line.

All of these discoveries are great examples of quality craftsmanship, but with a fresh, modern and relevant approach: perfect for Liberty.

Liberty, above all else, is about truly beautiful things. People come to the store to find things that are unique and special, and to me there are few things more special than Manolo Blahnik shoes.

Manolo is a true craftsman and is based in London. I had witnessed his popularity first-hand in the US where his personal appearances at Bergdorf Goodman drew hundreds of fans every time. He's a consummate gentleman and will always spend hours at these events, tirelessly autographing shoes, arm casts, boobs, anything. He's gracious with the crazies and loved by all who meet him. Personally, I also admire his principles. Over the years, heel heights have rocketed with platforms allowing women to wear six-inch heels. Designers, riding the shoe boom, have gone wild, creating ever more towering and painful styles to tap this lust, but not Manolo. He always thought these creations were vulgar and that the highest heel should be 4½ inches at most. He thinks the arch of the foot and the leg look more elegant that way and has never apologized for it, which is to be admired because he could have made a lot of money if he had made heels higher. But he's always stuck to his principles.

In 2010 – oddly, and despite having a huge presence in the US – the only place Manolo Blahnik was selling shoes in the UK was from his Chelsea store. It wasn't exactly on a retail thoroughfare, either. His boutique is tucked away on Church Street, a tiny street just off King's Road, beloved of locals but hidden from most of the world. This seemed insane to me. There was a huge dormant market in the UK, waiting for his designs.

It wasn't easy. Manolo had been through some bad experiences with department stores, but we started out by suggesting a collaborative capsule collection. Manolo happened to love Liberty prints, so we won him over. The collection launched in a pop-up in 2010 and was a huge success (naturally, a million fans and students showed up). After this, it was a slow process of charm attrition. The pop-up space, 'The World of Manolo', sold his shoes, bags and illustrations. Later on, we continued to work with Manolo, hosting book signings and Fashion's Night Out appearances. We have since established a permanent Manolo Blahnik department at Liberty.

That first Manolo collection marked the onset of a true festival of shoes at Liberty. At that time, the global love affair with designer footwear – the more outrageous the better – was still on trajectory. In November 2010 we decided to launch a special 'Shoe Weekend', with guest designer appearances from Nicholas Kirkwood, open Q&As with Rupert Sanderson, Raphael Young and Marc Hare, founder of men's shoe label Mr Hare. We ran with it, offering tutorials in high-heel walking and disco dancing. We even threw in free foot treatments from our foot spa.

It was just like the Henri Bendel days – create a convivial party scenario, and she will come. Even better: she will come, and she will shop.

Parties have become a tradition at Liberty, and something I have actively encouraged. They rock the foundations of the old broad.

We held a party for fashion designer Olivier Theyskens for the launch of his book, *The Other Side of the Picture*. It stands out to me, because Olivier was between jobs at Nina Ricci and his new role at Theory, and yet the fashion crowd came out in force to support him. Sarah Mower, Richard Nicoll, Nicholas Kirkwood, Rupert Everett, George Lamb, Meg Matthews, Derek Blasberg, Tim Blanks, Jonathan Saunders, Michael van der Ham, Susie Lau (Susie Bubble), Ben Kirchhoff, Ed Meadham, Lara Bohinc, and a bunch of other buyers, editors and stylists. (You see? Fashion people can be nice!)

One of our best parties at Liberty was when Katie Grand, editor-in-chief of *Love* magazine, collaborated with Alexander Wang on a special androgyny issue. Wang was one of our hottest designers at the time, and was already a fan of Katie's, so I suggested they host a launch party in the store during fashion week in 2011. Everyone came. Wang of course, and Katie, but also Pixie Geldof and Alexa Chung, Nick Grimshaw, Alison Goldfrapp, Alison Mosshart, Amber Rose, Daisy Lowe, La Roux, Erin O'Connor, Fred Butler, Nick Rhodes, The XX, Holly Johnson. At my request, Beth Ditto performed 'I Will Always Love You' by Whitney Houston, a cappella, and brought the house down. Boy George, and Victoria and David Beckham also came. It was *the* party of fashion week, rammed to the rafters with that amazing intangible sense of buzz you get from a great event. And we were responsible for it.

Our launch of Kenzo, later in 2012, was another triumph as far as Liberty's parties go. Kenzo was then at the early stages of its rebirth under Humberto Leon and Carol Lim (the masterminds behind the concept store Opening Ceremony). We staged a party at Liberty and it was packed with London's coolest fashion kids. There was a hot DJ and Daisy Lowe, Matthew Stone, Leigh Lezark, Henry Holland, Anna Laub, Miroslava Duma, Susie Lau and Jaime Perlman attended. Humberto and Carol had also secured their friend, the incredible music performance artist Blood Orange, to do a live show, which had everyone spellbound.

Then there's the Josh Wood launch party held the same year. Josh Wood, a hair stylist, is a celebrity in his own right in London and had become famous for taming the tresses of Gwyneth Paltrow, Laura Bailey and Elle Macpherson from his Notting Hill salon. Now he was launching another, in Liberty. To celebrate his arrival, we decided to go bold, and by that I mean outrageous. We decided to play with the idea of total glamour, so Josh hired a troop of drag queens to perform to disco classics, lip-syncing in an incredible performance on stage and also from the balconies, all clad in red evening gowns and blonde wigs. Laura Bailey came, of course, as did Kristen McMenamy. We capped the night by firing jets of red glitter confetti over everyone, from the top balcony. People rarely dance at fashion or beauty launches, but the disco mood had got hold of everyone. The crowd was spinning to Gloria Gaynor, The Emotions, and Earth, Wind and Fire late into the night.

I've also got to meet a fair few of my heroes through both parties and events at Liberty. A high point was meeting Prince Charles at a cocktail party for London Men's Fashion Week in 2012 at St James's Palace. Charles was the consummate party professional. I have never seen anyone work a room like it – he should write a book on etiquette. He did not leave the room until he had spoken to everyone, and in conversation he was utterly compelling. He looked you right in the eye and seemed very genuine. He told me how much he loved Liberty, and we had a laugh about how I was steadily becoming British in my behaviour, despite being a born-and-bred New Yorker.

Another thing we've ramped up at Liberty is our windows. Window displays are one of the biggest draws to the store, fundamental to creating buzz around what's inside, as well as creating inspiring stories around your product. There's a reason why people, including me, say 'put the goods in the window'. They are a key marketing channel, a theatrical stage set in which to communicate not only the magic of your store, but humour, spectacle and directionality.

Liberty has always been known for its windows, but we've really taken them to new levels in recent years, using them to tie in with current events in London from the Olympics to the tennis, to reinforce our ties to artists and craftsmen from around the world, and also to show our sense of humour.

We've had some crazy, brilliantly funny windows in my time at Liberty. For the royal wedding in 2011, we put the back of a real Mini Cooper car in the window, emblazoned with 'Just Married' stickers and surrounded with cake, bunting and corgis. Once, for London Fashion Week, we made a fake retro Hawaiian Motel set, with models strewn across tiki bars and hotel beds.

Despite Liberty's heritage building, we've also never been afraid to be modern or to use technology. For the Nike X Liberty running collection launch in 2012, we devoted every single window to a high-impact, continuous futuristic neon display, with the shoes suspended, seemingly in motion, with giant kinetic sculptural 'swooshes' following behind them. The glowing yellow orb attracted customers to the store both day and night.

One area in which I felt that Liberty was always underselling itself was beauty, and over the years Liberty's beauty buyer Gina Ritchie and I did something about it. Gina, a pretty girl with straight, honey-coloured hair and big eyes, earned her stripes at Harrods before joining Liberty. We got along immediately because she, like me, is a beauty junkie, and was also keen to sweep out some of the dead wood in the department. By the time we were done, the beauty department was totally transformed. (Gina is a shrewd merchant with an excellent skill for sourcing exciting brands that fit the Liberty mould. She's since expanded her remit from beauty to overseeing the accessories and jewellery departments.)

You had to see the 'before' to appreciate the 'after' in Liberty's beauty hall. Our ground floor, until that point, had been taken up with gifts, scarves and cards – plenty of affordable knick-knacks for people to buy – but the beauty department was comparatively tiny. And yet, at the time, the appetite for premium beauty and fragrance was huge. Not only that, there was a huge appreciation for niche brands. In the Regent Street and Oxford Street landscape, beauty retail was defined by department stores and uniform glowing concessions. There was nobody in this high-traffic area – populated by tourists, shoppers, workers and fashion press – that sold all the hot new, emerging brands.

That was it. We doubled the size of the beauty hall on the ground floor, from 2,500 square feet to 5,000 square feet, adding Trish McEvoy, Bobbi Brown, Dermalogica, Decléor, Byredo, Bumble and bumble, Hourglass Cosmetics, Aromatherapy Associates, and Chantecaille. It was Gina's genius idea to open up the store display windows surrounding the department, which previously featured shelves, allowing natural light to flood the area, while also providing an inviting honeypot for passing customers. We set colourful Hungarian tiles into the wooden floors, commissioned a hand-painted peacock mural by artist Kerry Lemon, and put in chandeliers made from lampshades in Liberty fabric. It was transformed. Today the beauty department is a constantly buzzing hive of activity, with customers sampling products, getting their makeup done, and lifting up bell jars to sniff artisanal candles.

Gina instilled a policy when relaunching Liberty's beauty department. While we had a few concessions from major beauty brands, in order to get away from that overwhelming familiar spaceship feeling, we restricted each brand to an equal-size plot. It ruffled a few feathers, and I got a few phones slammed on me, again, but the result has been an incredible beauty department where no brand is overly dominant. It's a lovely ecosystem of niche and bigger brands that complement each other.

All of the sales assistants know all of the product ranges and will advise in an unbiased way. They only give advice if asked and the policy is 'no hard sell'. This has also been really important to the success of our beauty department. Part of the reason so many people shop online for beauty, in spite of the fact that it's such a visceral, experiential product, is that the in-store experience for beauty is so pressured now. Visit any counter and you are pounced on immediately.

Consumers don't want to talk to sales assistants wearing a single brand's required eight eye shadow shades on their face, telling them what they should buy, and that it should only be from their brand. Nor do they want to be told a product is a miracle worker. There are no miracles. There is no magic goop! (Sorry everyone. There is no skincare item that will reverse the passage of time, or stop it, sadly. There is no makeup on earth that can change your face entirely.)

What we have emphasized at Liberty in beauty is, once again, only having the best. Gina handpicked the best items and brands within every category. She only agreed to stock it if we loved it. If it was tweezers, she picked Tweezerman. If she picked a makeup brand like Chantecaille or Bobbi Brown, it was because she loved it. In doing this we killed two birds with one stone: we didn't need any hard sell, because the products sold themselves.

We also expanded fragrances in the new beauty department. Liberty has always been known for its perfume department, but we bought in rarer, specialist brands with cult followings, such as Byredo, Francis Kurkdjian and Vilhelm while also extending the then-rocketing Parisian brand, Diptyque. By the time it was done, beauty was making 20 per cent of Liberty's total revenues (it was previously less than 10 per cent). We have also doubled our beauty volume from £10 million to £20 million pounds, in four years.

Fragrances at Liberty have also been a powerful tie for bringing in celebrities to the store. I remember immediately putting in a call when I heard Dita Von Teese was launching a fragrance. I met her for lunch at Claridge's to discuss it. She's quite mesmerizing to be around in person: incredibly sharp, but also very controlled.

We agreed that Dita would make a personal appearance at Liberty for the launch, and I promptly went to town on making it as glamorous as possible. Dita arrived on the day in a Rolls-Royce 1964 Phantom. We had a cast of gorgeous male models, clad in 1930s black tie, to pose next to her. We found a baroque, marble-fronted table for her to sign the bottles on. We then adorned everything in red roses. Fans (an army of Dita lookalikes) were queuing around the block for Dita who showed up in a forest-green draped Hervé L. Leroux dress, red lipstick, and with her signature jet-black hair perfectly coiffed.

Later, when we held a private dinner to celebrate the fragrance at the Arts Club in Mayfair, Dita let down her guard a little. Surrounded by her friends, Christian Louboutin, David Downton the illustrator, Stephen Jones, Roland Mouret and Lulu Guinness, she made a touching speech about how beneath the glamour she was just a girl from Michigan at heart. It was lovely – though despite the flowing champagne, she never once let a hair fall out of place.

We've had lots of celebrities through our door at Liberty. I remember the day that Will.i.am called our office (you can imagine Judy announcing that call! 'Ed! I have a Will I Am on the line!'). He was incredibly humble, and asked if he could come in to see me to talk about various projects he was working on. I was surprised by how nice he was, despite being so driven. We took him on a tour of the store and he even did a little shopping. Pharrell Williams also visited the store when his fragrance launched with us. He is completely charming and caused a sensation when walking around. I have to admit my shamelessness with him too – the moment he was free I asked to have our picture taken together. To which he gracefully obliged.

Then there was Richard E. Grant – who henceforth should simply just be known as 'the nicest man in showbiz'. When I first heard he was launching a fragrance my heart sank. Uck, not another celebrity fragrance! But it turned out Richard had devoted a lifetime to learning about fragrance, and was about as far away as you could get from Beyoncé (or Beyontz). He didn't want any trace of his face or name on it, to begin with.

The truth is, Richard is a fragrance obsessive. He'd spent years studying scent, and perfumery, and finally – as one does when one moves north of fifty – decided to take the plunge and do something about it. He wanted to create a fragrance but one that was not obviously 'Richard E. Grant'. He wanted it to stand on its own two feet, and he sought our advice.

It's impossible not to love Richard. He is so incredibly gracious, and responded like a true British gentleman when I delivered some pretty direct rounds of feedback in the early stages, and later – including that his packaging looked tomato-coloured (and not in a good way).

Richard E. Grant adapted, and worked closely with myself, Gina and Alienor Massenet, a renowned fragrance expert in the industry, for two years. The product, as a result, is fantastic. The fragrance, called Jack in reference to the Union Jack (collecting Union Jacks is another passion of Richard's), is a sophisticated unisex scent, with earthy and citrus notes. There are top notes of smoke, marijuana and mandarin, middle notes of pepper and clove, and base notes of warm oud, tobacco and white musk. Richard launched the fragrance in-store with a great Liberty bash, inviting his friends, artist Tracey Emin, Poppy Delevingne, Daisy Bevan, Bob Geldof and Matthew Williamson to come along, himself clad in a vintage military Union Jack jacket. Jack really does stand on its own two feet, and he's subsequently gone on to create another fragrance.

Besides beauty, another area of Liberty's ground floor that we have worked to maximize is jewellery. Women have for eons come to Liberty for incredible costume jewellery, and in the years before I joined, Liberty designer costume jewellery and fashion fine jewellery had exploded as a category, with every luxury brand introducing £2,000 necklaces dripping with ribbons and feathers.

It seemed to me a perfect opportunity to marry Liberty's tradition for 'special' products with its emphasis on craftsmanship and design, as jewellery is all about craft and storytelling. So we embarked on a major overhaul of the jewellery floor, arduously reconfiguring with new cabinets to add extra space (remember those protected beams).

We changed the department to reflect the wider shifts in the ways women now shop for jewellery. The idea of getting out jewels from the vault, and of giant diamond rings being bought by men for women apart from as engagement rings, is no longer relevant – save for the very, very lucky Kim Kardashian. Today, a new breed of affluent, professional women shop for jewellery for themselves. Such a woman will splurge on fine, or semi-fine jewellery, if she likes the design and the story, or she'll buy a statement costume piece to go with her handbag. The point is, she sees jewellery alongside accessories as an informal investment purchase, like a handbag or pair of shoes – not a once in a lifetime purchase, or something she buys as an heirloom. As such the price point is not in the millions but in the more comfortable zone of £600 to £6,000, which, trust me, tots up quite nicely when it's being bought more regularly than heirlooms.

The new kind of affluent female jewellery customer will also wear her purchases every day, with jeans or a dress. What she looks for is a story. Where jewellery has been dominated by quite conservative designs that are all about the stone, today women are more interested in the designer. They want to know who created it, what their background is, and how it was made. Plus they want it to be unique. They don't want the same identical, singular design that gets rolled out in a million different iterations.

The buying team and I have worked that approach to the maximum in Liberty's jewellery department. Our newly reconfigured jewellery emporium includes a host of new brands, including Anna Sheffield, Arman by Arman Sarkisyan, Daimyo, Eva Fehren, Fabrizio Riva, Larkspur & Hawk, Moritz Glik and Nak Armstrong. Many of these are from New York, which has become a hotbed for brands in this category (and provides another excuse for me to visit). The new department has been incredibly popular. My aim is for jewellery to rise from 15 per cent to 25 per cent of Liberty's sales before I leave.

Next up was homewares. This area is led by Liberty veteran Julie Hassan – a warm, funny, hilariously dry merchant with a killer eye. Again, our wit has come in. We wanted the department to be like a chocolate box, with quirky items as well as beautiful handcrafted objects and ceramics. We have artist Rory Dobner's ceramic tiles and candleholders, featuring his original black-and-white ink drawings. There's a corner dedicated to the Parisian home interiors and tableware store Astier de Villatte (another first in the UK and exclusive to Liberty). Meanwhile, we've thrown in some kitsch: from House of Hackney pineapple lights to retro ceramic poodle lamps, which have become surprise bestsellers. House of Hackney, a cult east London homewares label, is fawned over by hipsters for its quirky, surreal prints, vibrant velvet cushions, exotic floor lampshades and mugs. It's been so popular we recently launched a House of Hackney shop-in-shop at Liberty.

Part of successful retailing involves telling stories; I've always believed that. Any product you stock, any event you have, must have a story – just like Richard E. Grant's. You have to have something to talk about and create your own news to be noticed. I'd found a way to do that through parties, collaborations and in-store events.

But there was one medium I hadn't yet explored for putting Liberty back on the map: TV.

That was, until Kate Brindley, our head of marketing and communications, suggested it. I met Kate – otherwise known as the force of nature – on the first day I arrived at Liberty and immediately could tell she was sharp. She's nice too, which is something of an anomaly in the world of retail PR. She understands the Liberty brand and knows exactly which events or collaborations are right for us. She is funny and vivacious, with brown curly hair, a great eye for detail and a fearless love of fashion (never to be seen at an event without high heels and a statement dress – all the better if it's body con). Kate's also taught me to be bolder and to laugh off the headlines. They are great publicity, after all.

Liberty, with its jaw-dropping store and amazing stories, was made for television; very early on, Kate encouraged me to explore this. The store exudes personality. One of my early outings at her behest was *Britain's Next Big Thing*, starring entrepreneur Theo Paphitis (he of *Dragon's Den* fame). The concept of the show was simple, and very similar to Liberty's own Open Call platform. Budding product designers and entrepreneurs would come along and pitch their ideas to Habitat, Liberty or Boots and be judged on their commercial viability – the ultimate prize being that their product was stocked in one of the stores. Among the guest judges, I was cast as the 'Simon Cowell', the Mister Nasty who gave it to people straight, which is hilarious because I'm frequently accused of being too nice! All the same, it was fun, and a terrific vehicle for Liberty. Me, the US import, on Britain's great BBC.

That one television show, which aired in autumn 2011, unlocked a floodgate of attention on Liberty. In 2012, I was asked to appear on *The Apprentice* on BBC2 as a judge, meeting Lord Sugar (more British TV royalty). I first had to pose as a mystery shopper, quizzing the teams about their product, before delivering some rapid-fire retail questions and harsh feedback when they tried to pitch it to me as a buyer.

It was a strange sensation to see myself on television. I've never quite got used to it. They always seem to focus in on my most embarrassing sound bites. I remember, for *The Apprentice*, the advertisements for the show featured a clip of me looking angry and shouting: 'I'm confused!' The staff at Liberty had fun with that one. For days after the adverts aired, I had buyers and sales assistants turning to me exclaiming: 'I'm confused!'

Theo Paphitis and Lord Sugar were just the beginning, though.

In 2013, Liberty hit the big time: we were to star in our own three-part documentary on Channel 4, *Liberty of London*. The show would chart our run-up to Christmas in the busy winter shopping season. The response to this show was unprecedented.

We get approached at Liberty all the time about appearing on shows, but I have come to learn you really have to be careful before agreeing to these things. If you don't work with the right production company, you can be stitched up and edited to look like a bunch of idiots, or it can be cheesy. Either way, it backfires. And even I have bosses to answer to if Liberty becomes a laughing stock. But at the same time, television also offers terrific exposure for a store.

There will always be pundits commenting snarkily on your appearances on TV (I seem to remember a delightful, and rather bigoted, review of *Britain's Next Big Thing* in the *Spectator* entitled 'Carry on Camping' – in reference to me. 'Ed is camp. Very camp. There is Camp coffee, scout camp and there is Ed.' Ha!) But thus far, our forays on television have been well received.

The fact is, as I've said before, people love Liberty. Our products and our store are beautiful, and we've got charm. Rize, the Los Angeles production company behind the hugely successful BBC2 three-part documentary *Inside Claridge's*, seemed the right fit. *Inside Claridge's* struck a great balance between celebration and affectionately revealing idiosyncrasies in the iconic Mayfair institution, while also – in the personal stories and behind-the-scenes detail – showing all the love and effort that goes into running a luxury hotel of that nature. We agreed to take part in filming, exposing Liberty to the cameras in the run-up to our most critical period at Christmas.

Appearing on a show is different to being the star of one, and nothing had really prepared us for cameras being present in Liberty all day, every day, for several months. But the staff were pros and by the time the filming ended they barely noticed them there. The crew regularly filmed my cab rides in from work, or between appointments. I remember I had to start getting up even earlier than my usual 6 a.m. so that I could prepare, especially if they were filming at my house. I need two strong black coffees, and two cigarettes before I can face the world, so this ritual began at daybreak.

What I loved most about the show was the sense of affection, for both the store and my staff. Judy Rose, our eccentric but lovable receptionist, is seen talking about what makes Liberty so special, and also leading charity drives. Lee Whittle – our general manager – is shown frequently delivering the hilarious deadpan one-liners. (His attention to detail is also shown, from checking railings, to stock replenishment, to untidy stockrooms.)

The incredible people behind the scenes at Liberty are also featured, such as Emma Mawston, our head of Liberty Art Fabrics, and Julie Hassan, our formidable home buyer, whose life, from 1 January all the way through to 24 December, is dominated by delivering sparkling Liberty Christmas joy to customers through the Liberty Christmas department.

Our Christmas window unveiling marks the finale of the show. They are revealed to the public with a big old party (obviously), featuring a gospel choir, a purple light show projecting moving images all over the Liberty facade, and windows with maximum sparkle delivered by our then-creative director, Maxine Groucutt. (I seem to remember being quoted as saying: 'My favourite colour is sparkly,' so maybe the *Spectator* was right, after all!) The sparkle was fantastic. Our windows were a triumph. The final shot is of all the staff together and near tears, because it was such a great moment.

I didn't quite emerge unscathed, though. God bless the *Daily Mail*, which ran a few large diatribes about the show, and made a few choice digs at Liberty's evil resident American.

I was more upset than I let on at the time, which is probably childish, but I don't think anyone truly gets used to such comments being made about them. You'd be weird if you didn't get upset. I'd taken quite a gamble letting cameras inside Liberty, and this coverage was nothing short of vitriolic. Meanwhile, the descriptions of me were so very far from how I set out to behave, or like to think I am. (Ask my staff as to its accuracy. There's a reason many have stayed with me for so many years, and it's not because I have them locked up cowering in a floral-printed cell.)

Thankfully, this response was fairly isolated – we got plenty of rave reviews. And, besides, we had the last laugh. The show received over 2 million viewers; it was Channel 4's highest-rated show on the day it debuted, and our sales went through the roof. Our staff became celebrities, footfall at the store was up 60 per cent, and in the weeks leading up to Christmas we had to marshal the queues in and out of the store from different entrances and exits because it was so busy. DCD Rights has since acquired the worldwide distribution rights to the series, and it has aired the show on Australia's Foxtel network and NRK in Norway.

Beyond the occasional negative story, being on TV has brought about some major personal benefits. It got my friend Danny back for one – my best friend from the Florida days, who left that fateful, memory-jerking voicemail on my office answerphone one day.

Danny had moved to London in the nineties, unbeknownst to me, and then out of the blue, on a work trip, he had spotted me on television. Right away, he called my office, suggesting we meet. Friendships like Danny's and mine are very special. Immediately when I saw his figure, with dark hair and tanned skin, appear around the corner from Liberty, all those memories of debauchery in Fort Lauderdale flooded back, despite not having seen each other for decades. Within two seconds we'd slipped back into our shorthand, laughing about the old days and our misdemeanours. Danny had been living in south London all this time. How odd, I thought, that we should reunite thousands of miles from the US. We stayed out late that night with several glasses of wine, and have since made meeting up a regular occurrence, though we are now too old for all that clubbing.

Christmas is one of those times when, thankfully, unless you well and truly fail as a retailer, you are guaranteed successful sales. But it hasn't always been that way with other global calendar or national events at Liberty. I remain scarred from the much-vaunted 2012 summer Olympics. The way it was sold to us was that it would be Christmas on steroids with all those extra visitors descending on the capital. Every London retailer embarked enthusiastically on collaborations, limited-edition products, and crowd barriers! Crowd barriers . . . In retrospect, and with the equation tragedy + time = humour, I can just about laugh. But only just. The Olympics turned out to be a disaster for London retailers. The problem was that the government had sent out major warnings to all Londoners to avoid central London because public transport and the crowds would be too much. So, dutifully, the British, who love a rule, stayed away (1.5 million worked from home during the games). But the problem was, so did the tourists. They ended up bypassing central London entirely and going straight to the Olympic Park, before returning to their cozy hotels. Oxford Circus, as a result, was a ghost town for the two-week duration of the games.

Mercifully, this incident only stands out in my history at Liberty because it was isolated. The years 2010 to 2013 were all killers at Liberty, and the store really has blossomed. Each year, I've only truly stopped on Christmas Eve, before flying out to see my parents in Florida on Christmas Day – empty Christmas Day flights, with a glass of champagne in one hand and a novel in the other, are an underrated luxury.

In fact, since BlueGem has taken over, Liberty's success, as a shop and company, has soared. Annual sales in 2014 reached £124 million. Since 2010, our compound annual growth rate has been 16 per cent. Meanwhile, our store sales rose 11.2 per cent between 2013 and 2014 – thanks in part to our television show. We recently got minority investment to drive that growth even further.

Since Liberty has returned to its former glory, we've also been able to revive a few projects that were abandoned when they weren't doing so well, chiefly the Liberty luxury brand, which beyond our fabrics has huge potential as a stand-alone label. We've launched an in-house accessories line, Liberty London, designed by our creative team led by James Millar, made up of patterned, coated canvas bags, shoppers, wallets, scarves, sunglasses cases, neckerchiefs and rucksacks in bright colours, screen-printed by hand in Italy. They use our famous Iphis pattern, an art nouveau Liberty design, but have been brought up to date with vibrant pinks, turquoises and blues. They've been a hit already, and now even have their own shop on the ground floor.

I've found that one of the nicest things about working at Liberty is that the company truly celebrates the individual. Everyone who works there is unique, and is there because, on some level, they buy into the indefinable 'spirit' of the place. It's the kind of place that comfortably houses all sorts of personalities, like a collage, or indeed like a Liberty print. All those handmade, or hand-drawn, quirky details combine to create a beautiful vibrant picture when you stand back.

Bruce Lepere, our Oriental rug buyer, is one such character. Bruce, a middle-aged, bespectacled, antique-loving rebel, has worked at Liberty for decades and is the head of the Aladdin's cave that is our carpet department. He's extremely passionate about what he does, knows everything about rugs, and frequently travels the globe in Arthur Liberty's footsteps finding the most unusual and exotic homewares to bring back to Liberty.

Bruce has been his own man for his entire time at Liberty – the rug department is a concession. And when I arrived he was rather entrenched and understandably territorial. I don't think anyone had actually gone and spoken to the guy for a while. He was a little wary of me too, I think, because I seemed to be making a lot of changes in the store.

The way – I have found – to approach this kind of situation is to earn respect by showing that you know what you're talking about, making people trust you rather than simply barking orders. If they trust you, they will accept being led by you.

I also went in there and was honest about the fact that I knew absolutely zero about rugs. I listened to him talk about the rugs a lot, which was actually fascinating, before coming back with some suggestions. Over the years since I've been here we've slipped into quite a lovely working relationship, in which we frequently disagree on the prices (his pieces are so beautiful that I think he should often charge more for them), but ultimately respect each other.

Louis Matthewman is another example of a unique character, a Liberty devotee who daily sports a different bow tie, suit, and neatly combed hair to work, despite only being in his twenties. Louis started out as an events assistant at Liberty, and when I arrived he was already a tireless perfectionist in setting up any event at the store. I warmed to him because he is a good worker, extremely affable and funny, and has succeeded by consistently over-delivering on any task. Louis has risen up through Liberty and is now responsible for directing and orchestrating all events – logistics and execution, from the flowers to VIP care, to press lines.

From the moment you arrive in a business with a team already in place, there's a period where you assess their skill level – in other words, checking whether you will be managing imbeciles. But from the outset, when I joined in 2008, it was clear that the Liberty team didn't need me running after them saying, 'Pick the blue sweater!' They'd just lost a bit of confidence with all the changes. With the reintroduction of the psychiatrist sofa in my office (my padded chairs are upholstered in Liberty print and I also have a stash of chocolate), they've all excelled. In the first year, I was travelling to attend buying meetings 180 days out of the year. The next year I was travelling for ninety days, followed by thirty days the year after. Now, I just hang out at Liberty.

Which leads me to my wish list. I am a workaholic and am the first to admit it, but in my time in London I have developed a roster of places I have to see before I leave Merrie Olde England's fair shores. These include the Isle of Wight, Padstow in Cornwall, Whitstable and Margate in Kent, Snowdonia and the Outer Hebrides.

I have already visited St Austell in Cornwall with Scott, which was a rollercoaster in itself – two Yanks hitting the far West Country. To date, it is one of the most hilarious, and somewhat calamitous, weekends of my life. It took five hours by train, and another hour to get there – many a teacake and glass of wine were had. We arrived late, and were not able to get food at the hotel as the kitchen had closed, much to Scott's dismay . . . If service culture in London differs to New York, the divide is chasmic between New York and Cornwall. We were given short, sharp shrift by our surly bartender. Several cigarettes and glasses of wine later, and we were fine.

The trauma for Scott continued, though, not least on a bike ride I'd suggested, in which Scott was given the one broken bicycle in the shop. The cycle back from Mevagissey features a big hill, but Scott's brakes wouldn't work, causing him to hurtle down the slope and nearly crash. It was a comedy of errors. He didn't forgive me for a long time for that one. He'd have preferred the spa . . .

Surreally, we'd also arrived in Cornwall when the nearby town Truro was celebrating Cornwall Gay Pride. We took it as a divine sign and dressed in our most outrageous outfits to attend. The highlight of the evening was a Lady Gaga impersonator singing her full catalogue of hits, while speaking intermittently in a thick Cornish accent.

Padstow is next on my list. I have a cutting of a travel feature taped to the wall of my office, and often find myself sat at my desk wistfully looking at it between number crunching. It's become a fantasy symbol of my next life. The hotel in the picture, a rustic stone-built place called Prospect House on the bay, overlooks the quay. Boats are dotted around the glacial water and the sun is shining. I mentally step into this picture whenever I need a moment of calm.

I'm not one for contemplative moments, but I have found myself feeling nostalgic as I look over plans for the next rearrangement of Liberty's store and design its new three-year strategy. All of this was so unexpected. This whole adventure was supposed to be a short segue, not a seven-year love affair. But that's essentially what it's become. It's been amazing to see it work again, and made me realize how motivated I am by solving problems. I realized in many ways that problem-solving is my strong suit in retail. I find problems more exciting than successes because they are more interesting. It's more fun to keep twisting that Rubik's cube until it works again, than to arrive with it finished.

Which is why, of late, walking into a meeting in summer 2014 to announce and unveil my strategy to Marco, I was a little shaky and emotional. Would I be able to work without her? No more creaky staircases. No more buckets under leaking roofs, but no more quirky fabulousness either. The old spook house and I had become the best of friends.

At the same time, as many other people feel when they get to my age, I was getting this nagging need to plan my last career act. I have nothing left to prove in retail, but I knew I had one more challenge left in me.

I'm also of the belief that one should bow out before the very end of a party, gracefully, with a little dignity. I never liked the idea of being some doddering stalwart who refused to budge, trying to stay relevant. Better to leave on a high.

And then there was the siren call of New York. I adore London, and never see myself leaving her entirely, but the throng, dirt and energy of Manhattan were starting to tug on my heart-strings, and I needed to find some way to spend more time there.

Marco understood immediately why I was so torn. He knew I never really wanted to leave England behind. But I'm an American. How to have my British and American cake – and eat it too? His next idea was both genius and a giant relief.

Our new wholesale businesses were starting to get global attention – attracting customers from the US – and they needed managing!

He suggested I split my time and be based in both NYC and London. How simple and how clever.

I'd continue to do what I love, with people I love and respect, and in the places I love.

I'm going to have Broadway and Padstow – and that makes me the luckiest guy on the planet.

ACKNOWLEDGEMENTS

A giant thank you to my very dear friend Lucie Greene, who I thoroughly enjoyed writing this book with.

To Hugh, Adam and Simon for getting this rolling – and a reality!

And of course to Beverly, Jamie, Joanne, Madelyn, Alex, Robert, Erika, Matt, Matthew, Sarah and Rachel. I adore you all.

To all my American friends and my new British ones!

And last but not least to: P. J. D. E. E. T. S. R. P. J.
You know who you are!!

INDEX